# Low Ca

# Mediterranean Diet Cookbook

# Table of Contents

# Disclaimer



While the author has taken the utmost effort to ensure the accuracy of the written content, all readers are advised to follow the information mentioned herein at their own risk. The author cannot be held responsible for any personal or commercial damage caused by the information. All readers are encouraged to seek professional advice when needed.

# Introduction

The modern world of diets and nutrition seems very much like the media news cycle; there's one that's really popular and people forget about it till they see the next shiny object. However, there's one diet that has stood the test of time: the Mediterranean diet. It's not just a diet, it's a healthy way of life in many parts of Europe. It's a cultural heritage that has been passed down through generations. It uses fresh, seasonal ingredients that includes heathy fats, proteins and grains. The Mediterranean diet is a very sustainable diet, allowing for a wide array of meats and plants, while being extremely healthy at the same time.

In this cookbook, we explore the marriage of the popular Mediterranean diet with a low carb diet. By combining the best elements of both diets, we have a group of recipes that can keep you healthy without making you feel deprived. The low carb version helps you reduce blood sugar levels, increase weight loss and manage overall health.

## Benefits of the Low Carb Mediterranean Diet:

### *Increased weight loss*

The diet encourages the consumption of healthy foods and reducing or cutting off unhealthy processed foods. With calorie restriction and recommendation for higher physical activity, you will lose much more weight on the low carb Mediterranean diet if followed consistently.

### *Burns stubborn fat.*

The diet helps burn stubborn abdominal fat that is usually the hardest to lose. You will notice that you lose inches from your belly as you follow the diet guidelines, especially by avoiding added sugars and exercising regularly.

### *Improved insulin resistance*

Insulin resistance is one factor that makes it very difficult for some people to lose weight. With this diet, the calorie restrictions and increased metabolic function help address the issue of insulin resistance.

### *Encourages long-term health improvement.*

Unlike some diets that only recommend quick steps for quick results, this diet encourages long-term changes for permanent results. It helps develop healthy eating habits and more physical movement to positively impact overall health.

### *Reduces the risk of chronic conditions.*

Chronic conditions like heart disease are caused purely due to unhealthy food and lifestyle choices. You will greatly reduce the risk of developing such chronic conditions by losing extra weight, reducing insulin resistance, and improving metabolism.

### *Improve energy levels.*

Consuming a lot of processed food and sugar causes fluctuating energy levels. These foods get consumed fast and result in energy crashes every soon. This makes you feel tired all day and increases untimely hunger pangs, which leads to weight gain. With the healthy food recommendation on the low carb Mediterranean diet, your energy levels stabilize, and you can get through your day productively.

### *Improves physical health.*

The diet encourages regular physical exercise and helps you build this habit for the long term. Regular exercise makes your body much stronger and more flexible in the long run.

### *Improves mental well-being.*

One of the causes of stress and mental health issues is consuming processed foods. The ingredients in these foods cause a lot of hormonal fluctuations and result in issues like stress, anxiety, and emotional eating. By eating better, you can greatly transition from this unhealthy state to a happier and more peaceful state.

### *Improved gut health*

Consuming whole foods will restore gut health to its optimal status. The body needs a certain number of healthy bacteria and other enzymes to sustain overall health. Consuming unhealthy food affects gut health and prevents proper metabolic function, amongst other things. With this diet, your gut health will soon be restored.

## Low Carb Mediterranean Diet Food List

The diet recommends the following lists to help you decide what you should and should not be eating while following it.

### *Foods to eat:*

- Fresh Fruits. Includes apples, pomegranate, grapes, blueberries, strawberries, blackberries, etc.
- Green vegetables. Includes broccoli, asparagus, kale, zucchini, etc.
- Nuts and seeds. Includes walnuts, peanuts, almonds, cashews, pistachios, etc.
- Whole grains (in moderation). Includes oatmeal, quinoa, and brown rice.

- Healthy fats. Includes chia seeds, coconut oil, hemp seeds, flax seeds, olive oil, avocados, etc.
- Animal protein. Includes chicken, milk, cheese, beef, pork, and yogurt.
- Seafood. Prawns, tuna, etc.
- Legumes. Includes pinto beans, black beans, white beans, garbanzo beans, etc.
- Herbs and Spices. Basil, oregano, thyme, rosemary help to add taste without excessive sale or sugar.

Foods recommended in this diet are mostly whole and unprocessed. It is all about consuming quality ingredients that encourage lower cholesterol levels and reduce unhealthy fats. The foods are not very restrictive, making the diet easier to follow.

### *Foods to avoid:*

- Refined oils
- Refined grains
- Artificial sweeteners
- Added sugar
- Processed food (Includes sausages, packaged cereals, plant-based meat, etc.)

- Processed meats (sausages, bacon, deli meats etc.)
- Excessive sweets and deserts
- Excessive alcohol

Foods on this list are all linked to weight gain, increased inflammation, and other health issues. The diet is not strictly restrictive; anything can be consumed in moderation. However, avoiding these foods will allow you to see faster results on the low carb Mediterranean diet. Consuming such foods will only sabotage your efforts.

Additionally, these foods below are part of the regular Mediterranean diet, but in the low carb version, we got to avoid these.

- Processed Carbs. White rice, white bread etc.
- Starchy vegetables such as potatoes, corns and peas

# Breakfast Recipes

## Turmeric Latte

Serves: 1

Nutritional values per serving: 1 cup

Calories: 184

Fat: 6 g

Carbohydrates: 22 g

Protein: 10 g

**Ingredients:**

- 1 ¼ cups soy milk
- ½ tablespoon turmeric powder
- ½ teaspoon ground cinnamon
- 1 whole clove, crushed
- 1 teaspoon vanilla extract
- ½ teaspoon ground ginger
- a pinch of ground black pepper

- 1 date, pitted, chopped

**Directions:**

1. Place milk, spices, vanilla, and date in a blender and blend until very smooth.
2. Pour the mixture into a saucepan and place it over medium heat.
3. When it starts boiling, turn down the heat and let it boil gently for a few minutes.
4. Pour into a cup and serve. If you like it cold, cool the latte to room temperature.
5. Place ice in a tall glass. Pour the cooled latte into the glass and serve.

## Raspberry Smoothie

Serves: 1

Nutritional values per serving: 1 smoothie

Calories: 231

Fat: 14 g

Carbohydrates: 13 g

Protein: 14 g

**Ingredients:**

- ¼ cup plus 1/8 cup fresh or frozen raspberries
- ¾ cup unsweetened coconut milk or almond milk
- ½ medium avocado, peeled, pitted, chopped
- ½ teaspoon vanilla extract
- ½ scoop unsweetened protein powder

**Directions:**

1. Blend raspberries, milk, protein powder, avocado, and vanilla until smooth.
2. Pour into a glass and serve.

## Triple Berry Smoothie

Serves: 1

Nutritional values per serving: 1 smoothie without spinach

Calories: 183

Fat: 10 g

Carbohydrates: 17 g

Protein: 8 g

**Ingredients:**

- ¼ cup Greek yogurt
- ¼ cup frozen strawberries
- ¼ cup frozen raspberries
- ¼ cup frozen blueberries
- ½ medium ripe avocado, peeled, chopped
- 2 cups almond milk
- 2 handfuls spinach (optional)

**Directions:**

1. Blend avocado, berries, yogurt, milk, and spinach until smooth.
2. Pour into a glass and serve.

## Strawberry Avocado Smoothie

Serves: 1

Nutritional values per serving: 1 smoothie

Calories: 165

Fat: 14 g

Carbohydrates: 11 g

Protein: 2 g

**Ingredients:**

- 1/3 cup frozen strawberries
- ¾ cup light coconut milk
- Ice cubes, as required
- ½ medium ripe avocado, peeled, pitted, chopped
- ½ tablespoon lime juice

**Directions:**

1. Blend together strawberries, coconut milk, ice, avocado, and lime juice in a blender until smooth.
2. Pour into a glass and serve.

## Mango Avocado Smoothie

Serves: 2

Nutritional values per serving: 1 smoothie

Calories: 341

Fat: 30 g

Carbohydrates: 22 g

Protein: 4 g

**Ingredients:**

- 2 medium ripe avocadoes, peeled, pitted, chopped
- 6 tablespoons fresh lemon juice
- 2/2 cup fresh or frozen mangoes
- 2 cups water
- 1 cup plain, 2% fat Greek yogurt
- Mango slices to garnish

**Directions:**

1. Add mango, avocado, lemon juice, yogurt, and water into a blender. Blend until you get a smooth puree.
2. Pour the smoothie into two glasses. Garnish with a mango slice in each glass and serve.

## Sweet Potato Hash with Sausage and Eggs

Serves: 2

Nutritional values per serving:

Calories: 399

Fat: 29 g

Carbohydrates: 17 g

Protein: 15 g

**Ingredients:**

- 1 medium sweet potato, peeled, cubed
- 1 ½ tablespoons coconut oil, divided
- ½ medium onion, chopped
- 4 ounces bulk sausage, sugar-free, diced
- ½ small bell pepper of any color, chopped
- salt to taste
- pepper to taste
- smoked paprika to taste
- red pepper flakes to taste
- 2 eggs
- thinly sliced scallions to garnish

**Directions:**

1. Add ½tablespoon of oil into a cast-iron pan and place it over medium heat. Add the sausage when the oil is hot and cook until light brown, stirring often. As you stir, break the meat into crumbles.

2. Add onion and bell pepper and stir. Cook until vegetables are tender. Remove the pan from heat.

3. Place another pan over medium heat. Pour the remaining oil into the pan.

4. Add the sweet potato and stir it into the oil. Cook until brown on the outside, stirring occasionally.

5. Cover the pan and cook until the sweet potato cubes are fork-tender. Transfer into the pan with sausage.

6. Stir together the sausage and sweet potato. Add seasonings as well and mix well. Make 2 cavities in the mixture.

7. Crack an egg into each cavity. Place the skillet over medium heat. Cover the skillet and let it cook gently on low heat. When the eggs are cooked per your preference, turn off the heat and serve.

## Pesto Cauliflower Rice Breakfast Bowls

Serves: 2

Nutritional values per serving: 1 bowl

Calories: 438

Fat: 6 g

Carbohydrates: 17 g

Protein: 12 g

**Ingredients:**

- ½ medium head cauliflower, grated to rice-like texture
- ½ cup pesto
- ½ avocado, peeled, pitted, diced
- salt to taste
- pepper to taste
- 1 ½ teaspoons extra-virgin olive oil
- 1 cup chopped spinach
- 2 eggs

**Directions:**

1. You can either grate the cauliflower using a grater or do it in the food processor.
2. Pour half the oil into a pan and place it over medium heat. When the oil is hot, add cauliflower and stir. Stir often until there is hardly any liquid left in the pan.
3. Stir in the pesto. Transfer the cauliflower rice into two bowls.

4. Clean the pan and place it back over heat. Crack the eggs into the pan and cook the eggs sunny side up or as you prefer.
5. Season with salt and pepper. Place an egg in each bowl and serve.

## Sausage Potato Pie

Serves: 4

<u>Nutritional values per serving:</u> ¼ recipe

Calories: 242

Fat: 10.9 g

Carbohydrates: 12.8 g

Protein: 22 g

**Ingredients:**

- 6 ounces ground sausage
- ¼ cup milk
- pepper to taste
- ½ pound raw, shredded potatoes or hash browns
- salt to taste

- 4 eggs
- 1 cup shredded kale
- ¾ teaspoon Herbes de Provence
- ½ cup shredded cheese

**Directions:**

1. Set the oven temperature to 350° F and preheat.
2. Prepare a small pie pan by lining it with parchment paper.
3. Place a skillet with sausage over medium heat. Cook until the sausage turns brown, stirring on and off. As you stir, break it into crumbles. Turn off the heat.
4. Beat eggs in a bowl, adding salt, pepper, milk, and herbes de Provence, and whisk well. Stir in the hash browns, kale, 1/3 cup cheese and the sausage. Stir until well combined.
5. Pour the mixture into the prepared pie pan. Sprinkle the remaining cheese on top. Cover the pan lightly with foil.
6. Place the pie pan in the oven for 20 – 25 minutes or bake until it sets. Uncover and increase the heat to 400° F. Bake until the top of the pie is golden brown.
7. Cut into 4 equal portions and serve.

## Avocado and Egg Toast

Serves: 2

Nutritional values per serving: 1 toast

Calories: 260

Fat: 16 g

Carbohydrates: 20 g

Protein: 12 g

**Ingredients:**

- 2 slices whole-grain sourdough bread, toasted
- 2 large eggs
- olive oil cooking spray
- freshly cracked pepper to taste
- 1 small avocado, peeled, pitted, mashed
- 2 tablespoons milk
- salt to taste
- 2 tablespoons sliced green onion

**Directions:**

1. Spread avocado over the toast.

2. Beat eggs in a bowl, adding milk and seasonings.
3. Place a non-stick pan over medium-low heat. Spray some oil into the pan.
4. Add the egg mixture to the pan and stir until the eggs are cooked.
5. Divide the scrambled eggs equally and place them over the avocado layer. Garnish with green onion and some more pepper and serve.

## California Summer Vegetable Omelet

Serves: 2

Nutritional values per serving: 1 omelet without toast or fruit

Calories: 319

Fat: 20 g

Carbohydrates: 19 g

Protein: 19 g

**Ingredients:**

- ½ cup chopped zucchini
- ½ cup cherry tomatoes, quartered
- ¼ cup chopped cilantro

- 2 tablespoons water
- ¼ cup shredded Monterey Jack cheese
- olive oil cooking spray
- ¼ cup diced onion
- 1 ear of corn, use only the kernels
- 4 large eggs
- 1/8 teaspoon black pepper
- ½ small avocado, peeled, sliced
- ¼ teaspoon salt or to taste

*To serve: Optional*

- whole-grain toast
- fresh fruit

**Directions:**

1. Place a nonstick pan over low heat. Spray the pan with cooking spray.
2. Add onion and stir. Next, add zucchini and cook for a few minutes until the vegetables are tender.

3. Meanwhile, add corn, tomatoes, and cilantro into a bowl and mix well. Transfer the zucchini mixture to the bowl of tomatoes.

4. Clean the pan and spray the pan with some oil.

5. Beat eggs in a bowl, adding water, eggs, and seasonings. Add half the eggs into the pan and cook until the omelet is nearly set.

6. Scatter half the corn mixture on one-half of the omelet. Sprinkle half the vegetable mixture on one-half of the omelet. Fold the other half of the omelet over the filling. Let it cook until the omelet is completely cooked.

7. Transfer onto a plate. Place half the avocado slices on top of the omelet and serve.

8. Make the other omelet similarly.

9. Serve omelet with suggested serving options if desired as a brunch option.

## Cabbage And Eggs Breakfast

Serves: 1

Nutritional values per serving: Entire recipe

Calories: 267

Fat: 25 g

Carbohydrates: 2 g

Protein: 6 g

**Ingredients:**

- 1/8 medium cabbage, shredded
- 1/8 teaspoon salt or to taste
- ½ teaspoon garlic powder
- 1 large egg
- 1 teaspoon ground black pepper
- 1 ½ tablespoons olive oil

**Directions:**

1. Add 1 tablespoon of oil to a nonstick pan and place it over medium-low heat. When the oil is hot, add cabbage and stir on and off until the cabbage is tender and there is almost no moisture in the pan.
2. Stir in the salt and transfer onto a plate.
3. Clean the pan and place it over medium heat. Add the remaining oil and let it heat.
4. Beat egg in a bowl, adding salt. Pour egg into the pan. Do not disturb the egg for about a minute or until it starts setting.

5. Now, stir the egg to get medium-sized pieces of the egg.
6. Add cabbage, pepper, and garlic powder, and stir the mixture well.
7. Cook for a couple of minutes, stirring occasionally. Serve hot.

## Maple Pumpkin Pie Buckwheat Groats

Serves: 1

Nutritional values per serving: Entire recipe without toppings

Calories: 344

Fat: 30 g

Carbohydrates: 9 g

Protein: 10 g

**Ingredients:**

- ¼ cup raw buckwheat groats
- ¼ teaspoon pumpkin pie spice
- ¼ teaspoon maple extract
- 1/3 cup unsweetened almond milk
- a pinch of salt

**Directions:**

1. Combine buckwheat, pumpkin pie spice, maple extract, milk, and salt in a saucepan.
2. Place the saucepan over medium-low heat and cook until the buckwheat is tender, stirring often. If it is uncooked and there isn't milk left in the saucepan, add more milk or some water.
3. Serve warm with toppings of your choice.

## Chocolate Chia Pudding

Serves: 1

Nutritional values per serving: 1 bowl, without toppings

Calories: 259

Fat: 21 g

Carbohydrates: 13.9 g

Protein: 7 g

**Ingredients:**

- 2 tablespoons chia seeds
- ¼ cup coconut milk
- 1 tablespoon unsweetened cocoa powder

- ½ teaspoon vanilla extract
- ¼ cup water
- ½ tablespoon natural peanut butter

**Directions:**

1. Combine chia seeds and water in a bowl. Set it aside for 15 minutes to swell up.
2. Add coconut milk, cocoa, vanilla, and peanut butter into another bowl and whisk until smooth.
3. Add the chia seeds and mix well. Cover and chill until ready to serve.
4. Serve with your favorite toppings.

## Mushroom, Pepper, and Spinach Frittata

Serves: 6

Nutritional values per serving: 1 wedge

Calories: 108

Fat: 8 g

Carbohydrates: 3.68 g

Protein: 5.56 g

**Ingredients:**

- 5 large eggs
- Pepper to taste
- Salt to taste
- ¼ teaspoon smoked paprika
- 1/8 teaspoon chili powder or to taste
- ½ cup chopped mushrooms
- ½ cup chopped spinach
- ¼ cup diced green bell peppers

**Directions:**

1. Set the temperature of the oven to 350°F and preheat the oven.
2. Grease a small, round baking pan of about 6 inches with cooking spray.
3. Beat eggs in a bowl, adding salt and pepper to taste.
4. Add the vegetables, paprika, and chili powder and whisk well.
5. Pour the mixture into the baking dish. Spread the vegetables evenly in the dish if necessary. Place it in the oven.

6. Set the timer for 15 - 18 minutes or until the center is firm.
7. Cool for about 3 – 4 minutes. Cut into 4 equal wedges and serve.

# Lunch Recipes

## Beef and Butternut Squash Bowls

Serves: 2

Nutritional values per serving: 1 bowl

Calories: 353

Fat: 18 g

Carbohydrates: 23 g

Protein: 28 g

**Ingredients:**

- 1 tablespoon extra-virgin olive oil
- ½ teaspoon minced garlic
- ½ pound extra-lean ground beef
- 1 cup quartered Brussels sprouts
- ½ teaspoon Italian seasoning
- ¼ teaspoon salt
- ¼ teaspoon pepper

- 1/8 teaspoon red chili flakes
- ¼ cup beef broth
- ¼ cup chopped onion
- ¼ cup chopped red bell pepper
- 1 cup cubed butternut squash
- ¼ cup tomato sauce
- chopped parsley to garnish if desired

**Directions:**

1. Add oil to a pan and place it over medium-high heat. Add onion and cook for a couple of minutes when the oil is hot.
2. Stir in the garlic and cook for about a minute.
3. Next goes the bell pepper into the pan. Stir-fry for a minute or two.
4. Stir in the beef. As you stir, break the meat into crumbles.
5. When the meat is light brown, stir in the seasonings, tomato sauce, squash, broth, and Brussels sprouts.
6. Cook covered until the squash is cooked.
7. Distribute the mixture into two bowls. Top with some parsley on top and serve.

## Chicken Avocado Salad

Serves: 2

Nutritional values per serving: ½ recipe, without serving option

Calories: 277

Fat: 16.3 g

Carbohydrates: 9.3 g

Protein: 23.5 g

**Ingredients:**

- 1 chicken breast, skinless, boneless
- 3 tablespoons diced red onion
- 1 tablespoon chopped fresh cilantro
- 1/8 plain yogurt
- 1 ½ teaspoons lime juice
- ½ teaspoon pepper
- ¼ teaspoon salt or to taste
- ½ red bell pepper, diced
- ½ jalapeños, chopped
- ½ avocado, peeled, pitted, diced

- 1 tablespoon ranch dressing
- ¾ teaspoon garlic powder
- ½ teaspoon chili powder or to taste

**Directions:**

1. To make the dressing: Combine yogurt, garlic powder, chili powder, lime juice, pepper, and ranch dressing in a bowl.
2. Boil a pot of water over medium heat. Add chicken and salt.
3. When the chicken is cooked, turn off the heat. Remove the chicken with a slotted spoon and place on your cutting board. When it cools slightly, chop or shred into smaller pieces.
4. Add chicken, onion, cilantro, bell pepper, jalapeño, and avocado into a bowl and toss well.
5. Add the dressing and mix well.
6. Cover and chill for 4-5 hours for the flavors to set in.
7. Toss well before serving.
8. You can serve it as it is, over Bibb lettuce, or as a filling for sandwiches using low-carb bread or wraps.

## Refried Bean Tostadas

Serves: 3

Nutritional values per serving: 1 tostada

Calories: 177

Fat: 8 g

Carbohydrates: 20 g

Protein: 8 g

**Ingredients:**

- 3 corn tortillas (6 inches each)
- 6 tablespoons salsa plus extra to serve
- ½ tablespoon chopped fresh cilantro
- 1 tablespoon sour cream
- 6 tablespoons fat-free refried beans
- ½ cup shredded cheddar cheese
- ½ shredded cup romaine lettuce

**Directions:**

1. Preheat the oven to 400° F.
2. Grease 3 muffin cups with cooking spray. Place a tortilla in each cup and press it onto the bottom and sides of the muffin cup so that the tortilla gets the shape of the muffin cup.
3. Place in the oven and bake for about 8 minutes or until golden brown.

4. Distribute equally the refried beans and place them in the baked tostadas. Place 2 tablespoons of salsa in each cup over the beans. Finally, sprinkle cheese.
5. Place the tostadas in the oven and bake for 5 – 7 minutes until heated.
6. Garnish with cilantro. Place lettuce on top. Drizzle some sour cream on top. Place some more salsa on top, if desired, and serve.

## Avocado Egg Salad

Serves: 2

Nutritional values per serving: ½ recipe without serving options

Calories: 224

Fat: 18 g

Carbohydrates: 6 g

Protein: 11 g

**Ingredients:**

- 3 hardboiled eggs, peeled, coarsely chopped
- 1 tablespoon lemon juice
- ¼ teaspoon salt

- 3 tablespoons finely chopped celery
- ½ medium avocado, peeled, pitted, chopped
- ½ tablespoon mayonnaise
- 1/8 teaspoon pepper
- 1 tablespoon chopped fresh chives plus extra to serve

*To serve: Optional*

- lettuce leaves
- whole grain bread, toasted

**Directions:**

1. Combine eggs, lemon juice, salt, celery, avocado, mayonnaise, pepper, and chives in a bowl. Mash the mixture with a fork.
2. Taste a bit of it and add more seasonings if required.
3. Serve it over any of the suggested serving options.

## Mediterranean Chickpeas Salad

Serves: 4

Nutritional values per serving: ¼ recipe

Calories: 367

Fat: 26 g

Carbohydrates: 21 g

Protein: 14 g

**Ingredients:**

- 2 small tomatoes, diced
- ¼ red bell pepper, diced
- ¼ green bell pepper, diced
- ¼ yellow bell pepper, diced
- 1 spring onion, chopped
- ½ small cucumber, chopped
- 1/8 cup sliced black olives
- ½ cup cubed feta cheese
- kosher salt to taste
- pepper to taste
- ½ teaspoon chopped parsley
- 1 small clove garlic, peeled, minced (optional)
- ¾ teaspoon balsamic vinegar
- ½ tablespoon extra-virgin olive oil

**Directions:**

1. Combine bell peppers, parsley, olive, feta, garlic, cucumber, tomatoes, and spring onion in a bowl. Add seasonings, vinegar, and oil. Mix well. Cover and set aside in the refrigerator for the flavors to meld.

2. This salad is meant to be served cold.

## Beef Wraps

Serves: 4

Nutritional values per serving: 4 wraps

Calories: 375

Fat: 26 g

Carbohydrates: 6 g

Protein: 30 g

**Ingredients:**

- 3 tablespoons coconut oil
- 1 1/3 pounds lean ground beef
- ¼ cup chopped fresh cilantro
- ½ red bell peppers, chopped

- 1 small yellow bell pepper, chopped
- 1 small green bell pepper, chopped
- 8 cloves garlic, minced
- 2 teaspoons minced ginger,
- 16 large cabbage leaves
- salt to taste
- pepper to taste

**Directions:**

1. Boil a large pot of water over medium heat.
2. Add a cabbage leaf to the boiling water.
3. Remove the cabbage leaves after 30 seconds with the help of tongs and immediately immerse them in a bowl of cold water.
4. Let it remain in the cold water for about 3-4 minutes. Remove from the cold water and dry the leaf with a kitchen towel.
5. Repeat the process with the remaining cabbage leaves.
6. Meanwhile, add oil to a skillet and let it heat over medium heat. Add onion, beef, and bell peppers and stir. Cook until beef is brown.

7. Stir in the ginger, garlic, cilantro, pepper, cumin, and salt. Turn off the heat.

8. Divide the meat filling among the leaves. Fold like a burrito and serve.

## Taco Pasta

Serves: 3

Nutritional values per serving: 1/3 recipe, without serving options

Calories: 194

Fat: 13 g

Carbohydrates: 7 g

Protein: 16 g

**Ingredients:**

- ¼ pound ground beef
- 1 clove garlic, minced
- ¾ teaspoon ground cumin
- 1/8 teaspoon black pepper or to taste
- ¼ teaspoon kosher salt

- 1 tablespoon chili powder
- ½ teaspoon onion powder
- 1/8 teaspoon ground coriander
- ¼ teaspoon dried oregano
- ½ cup water
- ½ cup shredded cheddar cheese
- ¾ cup canned or cooked black beans, rinsed, drained
- 1 tablespoon tomato sauce
- ½ cup cooked, low-carb pasta
- 2 tablespoons sour cream

*To serve: Optional*

- avocado slices
- chopped cilantro
- sliced jalapeños
- any other toppings of your choice

**Directions:**

1. Follow the directions given on the package of pasta and cook the pasta.
2. Add beef into a pan and place it over medium heat. Stir often and cook until brown, stirring often. Make sure to break the meat into crumbles as you stir.
3. Stir in all the spices, tomato sauce, and garlic, and cook for a few minutes.
4. Stir in water. Cook until the mixture becomes thick.
5. Mix in the pasta and heat thoroughly. Drizzle sour cream on top.
6. Serve with any of the suggested serving options if desired.

## Pesto and Turkey Cucumber Roll-Ups

Serves: 3

Nutritional values per serving: 2 roll-ups

Calories: 104

Fat: 6 g

Carbohydrates: 5 g

Protein: 7.6 g

**Ingredients:**

- 1 medium cucumber, trimmed, unpeeled, cut each into 6 slices lengthwise
- 2 slices mozzarella slices, cut into ½ inch strips
- 1/3 bell pepper, cut into matchsticks
- salt to taste
- pepper to taste
- 1 ½ tablespoons homemade basil pesto
- 2 ounces deli smoked turkey breast, shredded
- 1/8 cup shredded spinach

**Directions:**

1. Place cucumber slices over a baking sheet lined with parchment paper. Dry the cucumber slices by patting them with paper towels.
2. A teaspoon of pesto is to be smeared on each cucumber slice. Divide the cheese, bell peppers, and turkey equally and scatter on each cucumber slice. Season with salt and pepper.
3. Roll the cucumber slices with the filling and place them upright on a serving platter. Fasten with a toothpick if desired and serve.

## Cauliflower Rice and Beans

Serves: 6 to 7

Nutritional values per serving: 1 cup

Calories: 132

Fat: 3 g

Carbohydrates: 23 g

Protein: 6 g

**Ingredients:**

- ½ tablespoon olive oil
- ¼ cup diced red bell pepper
- ½ can (from a 15 ounces can) black beans, drained
- ¼ cup fresh or frozen corn, thawed
- ½ teaspoon chili flakes
- 1/3 – ½ cup water or vegetable broth
- 8 ounces cauliflower rice or ½ medium head cauliflower
- ½ cup diced onion
- 1 large clove garlic, minced

- ½ can (from a 14.5 ounce can) fire roasted diced tomatoes
- 1 teaspoon ground cumin
- chopped cilantro to garnish (optional)
- salt to taste
- pepper to taste

**Directions:**

1. Cauliflower rice is cauliflower florets grated to a rice-like texture. You can use store-bought ones or grate the cauliflower with a grater or in the food processor to a rice-like texture.
2. Add oil to a pan and place it over medium heat. Add cauliflower rice, bell pepper, onion, and garlic and stir. Cook for a couple of minutes.
3. Stir in the red pepper flakes, cumin, corn, tomatoes, pepper, and black beans.
4. Keep stirring for a few seconds until you get a nice aroma.
5. Pour water and broth and stir. When it starts boiling, turn down the heat and cook until there is no liquid in the pan.
6. Turn off the heat. Garnish with cilantro.
7. Serve hot.

## Creamy Potato Soup

Serves: 3 – 4

Nutritional values per serving: 1 cup

Calories: 224

Fat: 11.8 g

Carbohydrates: 23.9 g

Protein: 7.4 g

**Ingredients:**

- 1 ½ tablespoons olive oil
- 1 medium carrot, trimmed, chopped
- ½ tablespoon minced garlic
- 1 cup chopped onion
- ½ cup chopped celery
- ¾ pound potatoes, peeled, cubed
- ½ teaspoon minced fresh rosemary or 1/8 teaspoon dried rosemary
- 1 ½ tablespoons whole-wheat flour
- ½ cup shredded cheddar cheese

- salt to taste
- pepper to taste
- 2 small bay leaves
- 1/8 teaspoon red pepper flakes
- 2 cups stock or broth
- 1/8 cup sour cream or yogurt
- chopped parsley or chives to garnish

**Directions:**

1. Pour oil into a heavy pot and place it over medium heat.
2. Add onion, celery, and carrot when the oil is hot and stir on and off until the vegetables are slightly tender.
3. Add rosemary, garlic, and seasonings and stir constantly for about 30 seconds.
4. Sprinkle flour over the vegetables and stir until the flour turns slightly brown.
5. Add a cup of stock and stir constantly until thick. Add remaining stock and keep stirring until well combined.
6. When the soup starts boiling, turn down the heat to low. Stir in the bay leaves and potatoes. Cover the pot partially and cook until the potatoes are soft.

7. Discard the bay leaves. Add sour cream and cheese and stir.

8. Taste a bit of the soup and add more seasonings if necessary.

9. Mash about half the potatoes or blend half the potatoes with an immersion blender. So the soup will be thick, with pieces of potato.

10. Ladle the soup into bowls. Garnish with parsley and serve.

## Grilled Chicken

Serves: 2

Nutritional values per serving: 1 chicken breast

Calories: 413

Fat: 25 g

Carbohydrates: 2 g

Protein: 42 g

**Ingredients:**

- 2 boneless, skinless chicken breasts (about 7 ounces each)
- 2 large cloves garlic, peeled, minced
- ¼ teaspoon dried oregano
- ¼ teaspoon freshly ground black pepper
- 3 tablespoons extra-virgin olive oil
- ½ teaspoon dried thyme
- ¾ teaspoon salt or to taste
- ¾ teaspoon grated lemon zest

**Directions:**

1. Place chicken breasts between 2 plastic wraps and pound with a meat mallet until it is ½ inch thick evenly.
2. Combine garlic, oregano, pepper, oil, thyme, salt, and lemon zest in a bowl.
3. Rub this mixture over the chicken and place in a bowl. Keep the bowl covered in the refrigerator for 4 – 8 hours to marinate.
4. Set up your grill and preheat it to high heat. Grease the grates with some oil.
5. Grill the chicken for 2 – 3 minutes on each side. You can broil in an oven or cook in a grill pan if you do not have a grill.
6. The chicken is not to be overcooked. Serve hot.

## Mediterranean Cauliflower Salad

Serves: 2

Nutritional values per serving: ½ recipe

Calories: 62.2

Fat: 0.6 g

Carbohydrates: 13.2 g

Protein: 3.8 g

**Ingredients:**

- ½ head cauliflower cut into very small florets
- 2 Roma tomatoes, diced
- 1 small red onion, finely chopped
- kosher salt to taste
- pepper to taste
- ½ bunch parsley, chopped
- ½ cucumber, chopped
- 1 small clove garlic, peeled, minced
- juice of a lemon
- 1 tablespoon extra-virgin olive oil

**Directions:**

1. Combine cauliflower, parsley, garlic, cucumber, tomatoes, and onion in a bowl.
2. Add seasonings, lemon juice, and oil. Mix well. Cover and set aside for a while for the flavors to meld.

## Pea Soup with Quinoa

Serves: 3

Nutritional values per serving: 1 cup, without toppings

Calories: 126

Fat: 3 g

Carbohydrates: 19 g

Protein: 7 g

**Ingredients:**

- ¼ cup quinoa, rinsed
- ½ medium onion, chopped
- 2 cups chicken broth or vegetable broth
- 1/8 teaspoon pepper
- ½ cup water
- 1 teaspoon olive oil
- 5 ounces frozen peas
- ¼ teaspoon salt or to taste
- toppings of your choice, like yogurt, parmesan cheese, etc.

**Directions:**

1. Boil water in a saucepan. Stir in the quinoa. Turn down the heat to low and cook covered until dry.
2. In the meantime, add oil to another saucepan and place it over medium-high heat. When the oil is hot, add onion and cook until soft.
3. Add peas and broth and let it come to a boil. Turn down the heat and cook until the peas are soft.
4. Blend the soup with an immersion blender until smooth.

5. Add quinoa and seasonings and heat thoroughly. Ladle the soup into bowls. Place the desired toppings and serve.

## Chicken and Rice with Spring Veggies

Serves: 3

<u>Nutritional values per serving:</u> 1 1/3 cups

Calories: 264

Fat: 11 g

Carbohydrates: 23 g

Protein: 21 g

**Ingredients:**

- 1 teaspoon extra-virgin olive oil
- ½ shallot or onion, finely chopped
- ½ teaspoon dried thyme
- 1 ¼ cups chicken broth or chicken stock
- ¼ teaspoon salt or to taste
- ¼ bunch asparagus, trimmed, sliced
- ½ cup halved snap peas

- 1 tablespoon chopped chives
- 1 teaspoon unsalted butter
- ¼ cup finely diced red bell pepper (optional)
- ½ pound boneless, skinless chicken breasts cut into bite-size chunks
- 1 cup quick-cooking brown rice
- 1 ounce cream cheese
- ½ cup fresh or frozen peas
- 1/8 cup shredded parmesan plus extra to serve
- 1 teaspoon chopped fresh tarragon

**Directions:**

1. Add oil and butter into a pan and place it over medium-high heat.
2. When the butter melts, add in the shallot.
3. Mix well and add thyme and red pepper. Mix well and cook for a couple of minutes.
4. Stir in the chicken. Stir occasionally and cook until the chicken doesn't look pink.

5. Stir in the salt and rice. Pour broth and stir. When it starts boiling, turn down the heat to medium-low and cook until there is less broth left in the pan.

6. Add cream cheese and stir. When the cream cheese melts, scatter the vegetables on top.

7. Cover the pan and turn down the heat to low. Turn off the heat after a couple of minutes. Do not uncover for about 5 minutes.

8. Add parmesan, tarragon, and chives, and stir the entire dish well.

9. Garnish with extra parmesan if using and serve.

# Dinner Recipes

## Turkey Sausage Zucchini Boats

Serves: 3

Nutritional values per serving: 2 zucchini boats

Calories: 240

Fat: 11 g

Carbohydrates: 13 g

Protein: 23 g

**Ingredients:**

- 3 medium zucchinis, trimmed, halved lengthwise
- ½ small onion, chopped
- 2 small cloves garlic, minced
- ½ teaspoon salt
- 1/8 teaspoon paprika or to taste
- ½ cup shredded part-skim mozzarella cheese, divided
- ½ pound lean ground turkey

- ½ celery rib, chopped
- ½ - 1 teaspoon Italian seasoning
- 1/8 teaspoon cayenne pepper
- ½ cup whole-wheat croutons, coarsely crushed

**Directions:**

1. Set the oven temperature to 350° F and preheat the oven.
2. Meanwhile, remove the seeds and some of the pulp of the zucchini halves. Leave about ¼ inch of the pulp all over. So now, these are your zucchini boats. Do not discard the scooped seeds and pulp.
3. Place a skillet over medium heat. Add turkey, celery, onion, garlic, Italian seasoning, cayenne pepper, pepper, and salt, and cook until the turkey doesn't look pink, stirring often.
4. As you stir, break the meat into crumbles.
5. Add ¼ cup of cheese, croutons, and pulp and stir. Let it cook for a couple of minutes.
6. Place the zucchini halves in a baking dish. Place the stuffed zucchini halves in the baking dish. Drizzle a little water all around the zucchini halves.

7. Cover the baking dish with foil and place it in the oven. Set the timer for about 30 minutes or until the zucchini is tender but not overcooked. Now, discard the foil.
8. Top with remaining cheese. Continue baking for a few more minutes until the cheese melts.

## Mediterranean Salmon and Vegetable Quinoa

Serves: 2

Nutritional values per serving: ½ recipe

Calories: 222

Fat: 4 g

Carbohydrates: 16 g

Protein: 32 g

**Ingredients:**

For the quinoa:

- ½ cup uncooked quinoa
- ½ English cucumber, deseeded, diced
- 1/8 cup finely chopped red onion
- zest of ½ lemon, grated

- ¼ teaspoon kosher salt
- ½ cup cherry tomatoes, halved
- 2 fresh basil leaves, thinly sliced
- 1 cup water

For the salmon:

- 2 salmon fillets (5 ounces each)
- 1/8 cup chopped fresh parsley
- ¼ teaspoon kosher salt
- ½ teaspoon ground cumin
- 1/8 teaspoon black pepper
- ¼ teaspoon paprika
- 4 lemon wedges

**Directions:**

1. Set the oven to broil mode and preheat the oven to high heat. Place a sheet of foil in a baking dish. Spray some cooking spray over the foil.
2. Meanwhile, cook the quinoa. For this, combine water, salt, and quinoa in a saucepan.

3. Place the saucepan over high heat. When the water starts boiling, turn down the heat and cover the saucepan with a lid. Cook until there is no liquid left in the saucepan.

4. Remove the saucepan from the heat and loosen the quinoa grains with a fork.

5. Cover the saucepan and let it sit for about 10 minutes.

6. Place the salmon in the baking dish. Combine salt, cumin, pepper, and paprika in a bowl and sprinkle over the salmon.

7. Place the lemon wedges in the baking dish near the salmon. Place the baking dish in the oven on the lower third position and broil for 8 – 10 minutes or until the salmon is cooked.

8. Combine a bowl of quinoa, cucumber, onion, lemon zest, tomatoes, and basil.

9. Garnish the salmon with parsley. Serve salmon with vegetable quinoa.

## Shrimp Puttanesca

Serves: 2

Nutritional values per serving: 1 cup shrimp mixture, without pasta

Calories: 228

Fat: 12 g

Carbohydrates: 8 g

Protein: 20 g

**Ingredients:**

- 1 tablespoon olive oil, divided
- 1/8 – ¼ teaspoon crushed red pepper flakes
- ½ small onion, chopped
- 2 cloves garlic, minced
- ¼ cup dry white wine or vegetable broth
- ½ tablespoon capers
- 1/8 cup minced Italian parsley
- ½ pound raw shrimp, shelled, deveined
- 1/8 teaspoon salt or to taste
- 1 ½ anchovy fillets, rinsed, finely chopped
- 1 cup grape or cherry tomatoes
- 1/8 cup coarsely chopped Greek olives
- low carb spaghetti or zucchini noodles to serve

**Directions:**

1. Add ½ tablespoon of oil into a skillet and place it over medium heat. Add shrimp and red pepper flakes and stir.
2. Cook until the shrimp are pink. Add salt and stir. Transfer the shrimp to a bowl.
3. Add the remaining oil to the same pan.
4. Add onion and cook for a couple of minutes when the oil is hot. Add garlic and cook for a few seconds. Stir in the anchovies and red pepper flakes. As you stir, break the anchovies.
5. After 2 minutes, stir in the olives, wine, capers, and tomatoes. When it starts boiling, turn down the heat to low and cook until thick.
6. Add in the shrimp and parsley and stir.
7. Serve hot over low-carb spaghetti or zucchini noodles.

## Chicken Alfredo Zoodles

Serves: 2

Nutritional values per serving: ½ recipe without optional vegetables

Calories: 243

Fat: 10 g

Carbohydrates: 6 g

Protein: 30 g

**Ingredients:**

- 2 thin chicken breasts, skinless, boneless
- 2 teaspoons olive oil
- 2 medium zucchinis, trimmed
- ½ teaspoon Italian seasoning
- ¼ teaspoon salt
- pepper to taste
- 2 small cloves garlic, grated
- chopped parsley to garnish
- ¾ cup nonfat cold milk
- ¼ cup grated parmesan cheese
- ¾ tablespoon whole-wheat flour or arrowroot starch
- 1 ½ cups frozen peas, broccoli, or spinach (optional)

**Directions:**

1. Make noodles of the zucchini using a spiralizer or julienne peeler.
2. Place a nonstick pan over medium heat. Add ½ teaspoon of oil and let it heat.
3. Season the chicken with Italian seasoning, salt, and pepper and place in the pan. Stir on and off when the chicken is cooked, about 5 – 6 minutes on each side. Transfer the chicken onto a cutting board. When it cools slightly, cut into slices.
4. Add the remaining oil to the pan. Add flour and keep stirring until roux is formed and the flour is lightly toasted. Pour milk into the pan, stirring constantly.
5. Keep stirring until thick.
6. When it starts boiling, stir in the garlic and parmesan. Add the zucchini noodles and frozen vegetables if using, and mix well. Heat thoroughly and serve garnished with pepper and parsley.

## White Chili Chicken

Serves: 4 – 5

Nutritional values per serving: 1 cup, without toppings

Calories: 219

Fat: 7 g

Carbohydrates: 21 g

Protein: 19 g

**Ingredients:**

- ½ pound boneless, skinless chicken breasts, chopped
- ½ tablespoon olive or avocado oil
- 1 ¾ cups chicken broth
- 1 teaspoon ground cumin
- ¼ teaspoon chili powder
- ¾ teaspoon cayenne pepper or to taste
- 1 clove garlic, minced
- 2 ounces canned diced chilies or use fresh diced chilies to taste
- 1 teaspoon dried oregano
- 1 ½ cans (14.5 ounces each) Great Northern beans, drained, rinsed, divided
- sliced jalapeño to taste (optional)
- ½ cup Monterey Jack cheese
- ½ medium onion, diced

- 1/8 teaspoon pepper or to taste
- ½ teaspoon salt or to taste
- a handful of fresh cilantro, finely chopped
- juice of a lime plus extra to serve

**Directions:**

1. Add oil into a heavy-bottomed pot and place it over medium-high heat.
2. Add onion and garlic to the hot oil and cook for a few minutes.
3. Stir in the spices. Keep stirring for a few seconds until you get a nice aroma, making sure not to burn the spices.
4. Mash half a can of the beans and add into the pot along with broth, chicken, green chilies, and remaining beans. Cover the pot and let it come to a boil.
5. Now turn down the heat and cook for about 20 minutes. Remove the pot from heat.
6. Take out the chicken with a slotted spoon and place it on your cutting board. When it cools, shred the chicken and add it to the pot.
7. Add cilantro and lime juice and stir.
8. Serve in bowls with extra lime juice, jalapeño slices, and any other toppings of your choice.

## Zucchini Noodles With Chicken, Spinach And Parmesan

Serves: 2

Nutritional values per serving: ½ recipe

Calories: 309

Fat: 16.5 g

Carbohydrates: 7.5 g

Protein: 32.1 g

**Ingredients:**

- 1 ½ chicken breasts, skinless, boneless
- ½ teaspoon garlic powder
- ½ teaspoon dried parsley
- ½ teaspoon dried rosemary
- ½ teaspoon dried basil
- ½ teaspoon dried thyme
- 2 tablespoons avocado oil, divided
- salt to taste

- pepper to taste
- 1 ½ large zucchinis, trimmed
- 2 cups baby spinach
- 1 clove garlic, minced
- 1/8 cup shredded parmesan cheese

**Directions:**

1. Make noodles of the zucchini using a spiralizer or a julienne peeler.
2. Set the oven temperature to 425° F and preheat the oven.
3. Brush a tablespoon of oil on either side of the chicken breasts and place in a baking dish.
4. Combine garlic powder, salt, pepper, and dried herbs in a bowl and sprinkle on either side of the chicken.
5. Place the baking dish in the oven and bake until the chicken is cooked through (the internal temperature of the meat in the thickest part should show 165° F on a meat thermometer).
6. Take the baking dish from the oven and place the chicken on your cutting board. When it cools slightly, cut into small pieces.
7. Add the remaining oil into a pan and place it over medium heat. When the oil is hot, drop the garlic into the pan and

keep stirring for about 30 seconds. Make sure you do not burn the garlic.

8. Place spinach in the pan. Stir and cook until the spinach turns limp.
9. Stir in the chicken and zucchini and heat thoroughly.
10. Divide the zucchini noodle mixture among 2 serving plates or bowls. Garnish with pepper and parmesan cheese and serve.

## Chickpeas Vegetable Barley Soup

Serves: 14

Nutritional values per serving: 1/14 recipe

Calories: 159

Fat: 5 g

Carbohydrates: 25 g

Protein: 5 g

**Ingredients:**

- 2 cans (15 ounces each) chickpeas, drained, rinsed
- 1 pound zucchini, julienne cut
- 10 ounces carrots, julienne cut

- ½ pound squash, julienne cut
- 4 cups chopped kale
- 10 ounces celery, chopped
- 2 inches ginger, peeled, julienne cut
- 1 ½ pound tomatoes, chopped
- 1 pound onions, sliced
- ¼ cup fresh lemon juice
- 1 cup barley
- 4 tablespoons olive oil
- 4 teaspoons salt or to taste
- 5 – 6 bay leaves
- pepper to taste
- 18 cups water
- 1 teaspoon chopped fresh rosemary

**Directions:**

1. Cook the barley as per the instructions given on the package.

2. Add oil to a soup pot. When the oil is hot, add bay leaves and ginger and stir. Cook for about 30 seconds until you get a nice aroma.

3. Stir in celery, onion, and tomatoes, and cook until the tomatoes are soft.

4. Stir in zucchini, carrots, squash, kale, salt, and pepper, and cook for a few minutes until slightly tender.

5. Add chickpeas, barley, and water. When the soup starts boiling, turn down the heat and let it boil gently for about 30 minutes. Stir occasionally. If there is no water in the pot, add some more water.

6. Stir in rosemary and lemon juice and turn off the heat.

7. Ladle into soup bowls and serve. Cool the remaining soup completely and store it in an airtight container in the refrigerator or freezer. It can last 4 to 5 days in the refrigerator or about a month in the freezer.

## Kale and White Bean Soup

Serves: 4

Nutritional values per serving: ¼ recipe

Calories: 181

Fat: 7.7 g

Carbohydrates: 12.5 g

Protein: 15.4 g

**Ingredients:**

- ½ tablespoon extra-virgin olive oil
- 1 small onion, chopped
- ½ medium carrot, chopped
- 1 bay leaf
- 1 cup water
- 1.5 ounces lacinato kale
- 7 ounces Polish kielbasa (turkey and beef), sliced diagonally
- 1 clove garlic, minced
- 2 medium stalks celery, chopped
- 2 cups chicken broth
- ¼ cup canned cannellini beans
- salt to taste
- pepper to taste

**Directions:**

1. Add oil into a saucepan and place it over medium heat.
2. Add the sausage and cook until brown on each side when the oil is hot.
3. Transfer the sausage to a bowl.
4. Add onion, carrot, garlic, bay leaf, and celery and stir. Add salt to taste.
5. Cook for a few minutes until brown.
6. Pour broth and water. When it starts boiling, turn down the heat and simmer until the vegetables are slightly tender.
7. Stir in seasonings, white beans, and kale. Heat thoroughly. Ladle the soup into bowls and serve.

## Creamy Skillet Ranch Chicken and Broccoli

Serves: 2

Nutritional values per serving: ½ recipe

Calories: 374

Fat: 26 g

Carbohydrates: 6 g

Protein: 29 g

**Ingredients:**

- ½ pound boneless, skinless chicken breast, chopped into bite-size chunks
- ¼ teaspoon pepper, divided plus extra to garnish
- 2 cups bite-size broccoli florets
- ¼ cup heavy cream
- 1 tablespoon mayonnaise
- ¼ teaspoon onion powder
- 1/8 cup chopped mixed herbs of your choice
- ¼ teaspoon salt, divided
- 1 tablespoon extra-virgin olive oil, divided

- 1 tablespoon water
- 1 tablespoon white wine vinegar
- ½ teaspoon cornstarch
- ¼ teaspoon garlic powder

**Directions:**

1. Season the chicken with half the salt and pepper.
2. Pour ½ tablespoon of oil into a pan and place it over medium heat.
3. Add chicken to the hot oil. Cook until brown on each side and cooked through inside. Stir once in a while.
4. Remove the chicken from the pan and place on a plate.
5. Pour the remaining oil into the pan. Add broccoli and water and cover the pan.
6. Cook until the broccoli is crisp as well as tender.
7. Remove the broccoli from the pan and place it along with the chicken.
8. Add cream, mayonnaise, onion powder, garlic powder, vinegar, cornstarch, and remaining salt and pepper in a bowl and whisk well.
9. Turn up the heat to medium-high heat. Add the cream mixture to the pan. Stir constantly until thick.

10. Add the chicken, broccoli, and herbs to the cream mixture. Mix well and heat thoroughly.
11. Garnish with some pepper and serve.

## Spicy Chicken and Chickpeas

Serves: 2

Nutritional values per serving: ½ recipe

Calories: 273

Fat: 8 g

Carbohydrates: 14 g

Protein: 35 g

**Ingredients:**

- ½ pound skinless, boneless chicken breast, chopped
- 1 clove garlic, minced
- ½ tablespoon lemon juice
- 1 tablespoon chopped parsley
- ½ teaspoon pepper
- ½ cup canned or cooked chickpeas, rinsed, drained

- ½ tablespoon olive oil
- 1 scallion, thinly sliced
- ½ teaspoon crushed red pepper flakes
- salt to taste

**Directions:**

1. Pour oil into a pan and place it over medium-high heat. When the oil is hot, add chicken, pepper, salt, and crushed red pepper and stir.
2. Cook covered until the chicken doesn't look pink any longer.
3. Stir in the chickpeas. Stir-fry for a couple of minutes.
4. Stir in the garlic and cook for another couple of minutes.
5. Stir in the scallions. When the chicken is cooked through, turn off the heat.
6. Add lemon juice and parsley and mix well.
7. Serve.

## Grilled Shrimp and Mixed Vegetables

Serves: 2

Nutritional values per serving: ½ recipe

Calories: 390

Fat: 29 g

Carbohydrates: 15 g

Protein: 20 g

**Ingredients:**

- 2 cloves garlic, minced
- 1 teaspoon chopped fresh oregano or ½ teaspoon dried oregano
- salt to taste
- freshly ground black pepper to taste
- 2 teaspoons finely grated lemon zest
- ½ teaspoon chopped fresh rosemary
- ¼ cup olive oil plus extra to grease
- ½ pound extra-large shrimp, peeled, deveined
- 1 yellow squash, cut into ¾-inch slices diagonally
- ½ small red onion, cut into 4 wedges
- lime wedges to serve
- 6 ounces zucchini, cut into ¾-inch thick slices diagonally
- ½ pound asparagus, trimmed
- 4 ounces assorted cherry tomatoes

**Directions:**

1. To make marinade: Add herbs, garlic, salt, oil, pepper, and lemon zest into a bowl and stir.

2. Place shrimp in a bowl. Pour 1 ½ tablespoons of the marinade over the shrimp and mix well.

3. Cover the bowl and refrigerate for 1 – 24 hours. Take it out of the refrigerator an hour before grilling.

4. Set up your grill and preheat it to medium-high.

5. Combine zucchini, asparagus, squash, and onions in a bowl. Add 1 ½ tablespoons of the marinade and toss well.

6. Fix the shrimp and tomatoes on separate flat metal skewers.

7. Grease the grill grate with some oil. Place the vegetables on the grill grate and grill until the vegetables are crisp as well as tender. Baste with remaining marinade while grilling.

8. Grill the shrimp and tomatoes as well. The cooking time will be different for the shrimp and tomatoes. The tomatoes should be charred, and the shrimp should be pink when cooked.

9. Place the skewers on a serving platter. Place lemon wedges on the platter and serve.

## Beef, Brown Rice, and Mushroom Soup

Serves: 3

Nutritional values per serving: 1 ¼ cups

Calories: 240

Fat: 6 g

Carbohydrates: 15 g

Protein: 29 g

**Ingredients:**

- ½ tablespoon olive oil
- ¼ cup finely chopped celery
- 14 ounces beef chuck
- ½ teaspoon chopped fresh thyme or ¼ teaspoon dried thyme
- ¼ teaspoon freshly ground black pepper
- 3 tablespoons uncooked short-grain brown rice
- 2 small cloves garlic, sliced
- 4 ounces carrots, chopped
- 2 cups chicken broth or beef broth
- 1/8 teaspoon smoked paprika
- 1 tablespoon tomato paste

- 2 ounces mushrooms, sliced

**Directions:**

1. Pour oil into a soup pot and place it over medium heat. Add garlic to the hot oil. Stir often until the garlic is light brown.
2. Stir in the carrot and celery. Cook until light brown. Transfer the vegetables onto a plate.
3. Add meat into the pot and cook until brown all over. Transfer the meat onto your cutting board. When it cools down, chop into ¾ inch pieces.
4. Add broth to the soup pot. Scrape the bottom of the pot to remove any browned bits that may be stuck.
5. Mix well with meat, thyme, pepper, paprika, and tomato paste.
6. Cook covered, on low heat, for about 20 minutes.
7. Stir in the rice and cook for about 15 – 17 minutes.
8. Stir in the mushrooms and the cooked vegetables and continue simmering for another 30 minutes.
9. Ladle into soup bowls and serve.

## Mango and Grilled Chicken Salad

Serves: 2

Nutritional values per serving: ½ recipe

Calories: 210

Fat: 2 g

Carbohydrates: 22 g

Protein: 30 g

**Ingredients:**

For the chicken:

- ½ pound chicken tenderloins
- 1/8 teaspoon pepper
- ¼ teaspoon salt

For the salad:

- 3 cups torn, mixed salad greens
- ½ medium mango, peeled, cubed
- 2 tablespoons balsamic vinaigrette or raspberry vinaigrette
- ½ cup fresh sugar snap peas halved lengthwise

**Directions:**

1. Preheat the grill to medium heat or broil in an oven.
2. Season the chicken with salt and pepper.
3. Grease the grill grate with some oil. Place the chicken on the grill and cook for about 3 to 4 minutes on each side and cooked through inside.
4. Place the chicken on your cutting board. When it cools, cut into 1-inch pieces.
5. Place 1 ½ cups salad greens on each plate. Drizzle a tablespoon of vinaigrette on the salad greens on each plate. Divide the chicken, mango, and snap peas equally and place over the salad greens.
6. Serve right away.

## Chicken Caesar Salad

Serves: 3

Nutritional values per serving: 2 cups

Calories: 306

Fat: 16 g

Carbohydrates: 10.3 g

Protein: 29.3 g

**Ingredients:**

For the salad:

- 1 ½ cups skinless, shredded roasted chicken
- ½ cup julienne-cut red bell pepper
- 5 ½ cups torn romaine lettuce leaves
- ¾ cup plain, whole-wheat croutons
- ¼ cup freshly grated parmesan cheese

For the dressing:

- 1 ½ tablespoons olive oil
- 1 teaspoon Worcestershire sauce
- salt to taste

- ½ clove garlic, minced
- 2 teaspoons fresh lemon juice
- 1 teaspoon Dijon mustard
- pepper to taste

**Directions:**

1. To make dressing: Whisk together all the dressing ingredients in a bowl.
2. Add chicken, bell pepper, and lettuce into a bowl and toss well.
3. Add dressing and toss well.
4. Scatter croutons and cheese on top and serve.

**Directions:**

1. Follow the directions given on the package of pasta and cook the pasta. Retain about ½ cup of the cooked water and drain off the remaining water.
2. Meanwhile, place a skillet over medium-high heat. Spray the pan with cooking spray.
3. Add sausage to the skillet. Cook until brown, stirring on and off. As you stir, break the sausage into bite-size chunks.

4. Stir in the garlic. When the raw aroma of the garlic has gone, add kale and the retained pasta liquid and mix well.
5. Cook covered until the kale turns limp. Add beans, pasta, cheese, and oil and mix well. Add salt and pepper and serve.

# Snacks and Desserts

## Carrot Smoothie

Serves: 1

Nutritional values per serving: 1 smoothie

Calories:

Fat: g

Carbohydrates: g

Protein: g

**Ingredients:**

- ½ large peeled carrot thinly sliced
- 1 tablespoon almond or cashew butter

- 1 ½ teaspoons grated ginger
- ¼ teaspoon ground cinnamon
- ¼ cup water
- Ice cubes, as required

**Directions:**

1. Blend together carrot, nut butter, ginger, cinnamon, and water until smooth.
2. Add ice and blend until very chilled.
3. Pour into a glass and serve.

## Broccoli Smoothie

Serves: 1

Nutritional values per serving: 1 smoothie

Calories: 237

Fat: 21.2 g

Carbohydrates: 12.9 g

Protein: 5 g

**Ingredients:**

- 0.7 ounce frozen zucchini
- 0.6 ounce chopped frozen broccoli florets
- 0.6 ounce frozen pumpkin
- ½ cup baby spinach leaves
- 1/8 avocado, pitted, peeled, chopped
- 3 tablespoons coconut cream
- ½ cup water
- ice cubes, as required
- 0.25 ounce almonds or cashews
- ¼ teaspoon ground cinnamon
- ½ tablespoon raw cacao powder

**Directions:**

1. Blend zucchini, broccoli, pumpkin, spinach, avocado, coconut cream, almonds, cinnamon, cacao, and water until smooth.
2. Add ice and blend until very chilled.
3. Pour into a glass and serve.

## Cucumber Smoothie

Serves: 2

Nutritional values per serving: 1 smoothie

Calories: 293

Fat: 20.7 g

Carbohydrates: 17.5 g

Protein: 17.5 g

**Ingredients:**

- 2 cups water
- 1 avocado, peeled, pitted, chopped
- ½ cup chopped cilantro
- 1 cucumber peeled, chopped
- 1 cup loosely packed spinach leaves
- ½ tablespoon of lemon or lime juice or more to taste
- 2 scoops collagen
- ice cubes, as required
- 2 teaspoons ground flaxseeds

**Directions:**

1. Blend water, avocado, cilantro, cucumber, spinach, collagen, flaxseeds, and lemon juice in a blender until smooth.
2. Add ice and blend until very chilled.
3. Pour into a glass and serve.

## Avocado Date Chocolate Pudding

Serves: 4

Nutritional values per serving: 1 bowl

Calories: 100

Fat: 2 g

Carbohydrates: 21 g

Protein: 2 g

**Ingredients:**

- 12 dates, pitted, soaked in water for 2 hours, drained, chopped
- 5 tablespoons raw cacao powder
- 1 ½ medium ripe avocadoes, peeled, pitted chopped
- 3 teaspoons vanilla extract or 1 vanilla bean, use only seeds

**Directions:**

1. Place dates, cacao powder, avocadoes, and vanilla in a food processor or blender and process until smooth. Scrape the sides of the bowl whenever required.
2. Divide the pudding into four dessert bowls or ramekins and chill for at least an hour before serving.
3. It can last for 2 to 3 days in the refrigerator.

## Vegan Strawberry Ice Cream

Serves: 4

Nutritional values per serving: ¼ recipe

Calories: 139

Fat: 6.7 g

Carbohydrates: 19.6 g

Protein: 1.8 g

**Ingredients:**

- ½ cup oat milk or soy milk
- ½ cup pitted Medjool dates
- ½ teaspoon vanilla extract or seeds of ½ vanilla bean

- ½ cup full-fat canned coconut milk
- 1 ½ cups frozen strawberries
- ¼ teaspoon beet juice powder (optional)

**Directions:**

1. Add oat milk, dates, vanilla, coconut milk, strawberries, and beet juice powder into a blender. Beet juice powder is just used as a coloring.
2. Blend until smooth.
3. Churn the ice cream in an ice cream maker following the manufacturer's instructions.
4. You can serve right away for a soft serve texture. Transfer the ice cream into a freezer-safe container for firm ice cream. Freeze until firm.

## Baked Pears

Serves: 4

Nutritional values per serving:

Calories: 78

Fat: 3 g

Carbohydrates: 13 g

Protein: 0.5 g

**Ingredients:**

- 2 large, firm pears, peeled, halved, cored
- ¼ inch ginger, peeled, grated
- ¼ teaspoon ground cinnamon (optional)
- ¼ teaspoon ground cardamom
- ½ star anise, crushed (optional)
- 1 tablespoon butter, melted plus extra to grease
- 1/8 cup pistachios, crushed (optional)

**Directions:**

1. Make sure the pears aren't ripe.
2. Set the oven temperature to 425° F and preheat the oven.
3. Grease a baking dish with some butter.
4. Combine spices and butter in a small bowl. Brush this mixture over the pear halves and place in the baking dish, with the cut side touching the bottom.
5. Bake for about an hour; turn the pears over every 20 – 25 minutes. Baste the pears with any of the juices in the baking dish.

6. Place pears in individual serving bowls. Spoon the cooked juices, if any, on each pear. Garnish with pistachios if using and serve.

## Celery With Cream Cheese

Serves: 5

Nutritional values per serving: 1/5 recipe

Calories: 35

Fat: 3 g

Carbohydrates: 2 g

Protein: 1 g

**Ingredients:**

- 3 stalks of celery were rinsed, dried with paper towels, and cut into thirds
- 1 ½ teaspoons everything bagel mix
- 2.25 ounces whipped cream cheese
- paprika to garnish

**Directions:**

1. Combine cream cheese and ¾ teaspoon of everything bagel mix. Stuff this filling into the hollow part of the celery.
2. Garnish with remaining everything bagel mix and paprika and serve.

## Crunchy Roasted Chickpeas

Serves: 4

Nutritional values per serving: 1/8 cup

Calories: 53.3

Fat: 1.3 g

Carbohydrates: 8.7 g

Protein: 2 g

**Ingredients:**

- ¾ cup cooked or canned chickpeas, rinsed, drained
- ¼ teaspoon smoked paprika
- 1/8 teaspoon onion powder
- ¼ teaspoon salt
- ¼ teaspoon ground cumin

- ¼ teaspoon garlic powder
- 1/8 teaspoon ground coriander
- 1/8 teaspoon freshly ground pepper
- 2 teaspoons olive oil

**Directions:**

1. Preheat the oven to 400° F. Grease a baking sheet with olive oil spray.
2. Dry the chickpeas with paper towels. Make sure they are completely dry.
3. Combine the seasonings in a bowl.
4. Spread the chickpeas on the baking sheet and bake for 15 minutes.
5. Now, take out the baking sheet. Bring all the chickpeas together on the baking sheet. Trickle oil over the chickpeas and mix well. Sprinkle the spice mixture over the chickpeas and mix well.
6. Spread the chickpeas once again and continue baking until crisp, stirring the chickpeas every 10 minutes.
7. When the timer goes off, switch off the oven and leave the oven door ajar. Let them cool completely.

## Celery and Peanut Butter

Serves: 6

Nutritional values per serving: 1 piece without toppings

Calories: 36

Fat: 3 g

Carbohydrates: 0.9 g

Protein: 2 g

**Ingredients:**

- 2 tablespoons peanut butter
- 2 medium stalks celery, cut each into 3 equal pieces

Toppings: Optional

- small, dried fruit like raisins, cranberries, blueberries, etc.
- shredded coconut
- roasted nuts
- any other toppings of your choice

**Directions:**

1. Fill the celery stalks with peanut butter, a teaspoon per piece.

2. Place the chosen toppings on top and serve.

## Hummus and Carrot Sticks

Serves: 3

Nutritional values per serving: 1/3 cup hummus with 1 carrot

Calories: 214

Fat: 10 g

Carbohydrates: 24 g

Protein: 6 g

**Ingredients:**

- ¾ cup cooked or canned chickpeas
- 1 tablespoon lemon juice
- 1/8 teaspoon ground cumin
- 3 medium carrots, peeled, cut into sticks
- 2 tablespoons olive oil
- ½ small clove garlic, peeled
- ¼ teaspoon salt

**Directions:**

1. Blend chickpeas, lemon juice, cumin, oil, garlic, and salt until smooth.
2. Pour into an airtight container and refrigerate until use. It can last for a week.
3. Serve.

## Fruit Salad

Serves: 3

Nutritional values per serving: 1/3 recipe

Calories: 63

Fat: 1 g

Carbohydrates: 15 g

Protein: 2 g

**Ingredients:**

- 1 star fruit, cut into slices crosswise (star-shaped slices)
- ½ cup blackberries
- 1 cup cubed, deseeded watermelon
- 1 tablespoon chopped fresh mint
- ½ cup raspberries
- 1 cup quartered strawberries
- juice of a lime

**Directions:**

1. Combine star fruit, berries, watermelon, and mint in a bowl.
2. Add lime juice and mix well.
3. Serve right away, or chill and serve later.

## Parmesan Cheese Crisps

Serves: 6

Nutritional values per serving: 1/6 recipe

Calories: 31

Fat: 2 g

Carbohydrates: 0 g

Protein: 2 g

**Ingredients:**

- ½ teaspoon dried basil
- ½ cup shredded parmesan cheese

**Directions:**

1. Preheat the oven to 350°F. Place a sheet of parchment paper on a baking sheet.
2. Make 6 equal portions of the cheese and place on the baking sheet, leaving a sufficient gap between them.
3. Press each portion until flat. Scatter basil on the cheese. Place the baking sheet in the oven and bake until crispy and brown around the edges. It should take around 5 to 7 minutes.
4. Cool completely and serve.

## Turkey Meatballs

Serves: 23

Nutritional values per serving: 1 meatball

Calories: 26

Fat: 1 g

Carbohydrates: 1 g

Protein: 5 g

**Ingredients:**

- 1 pound ground turkey
- 1 large egg
- 1 tablespoon onion flakes or onion powder
- ½ teaspoon salt
- ½ cup shredded zucchini, squeezed off excess moisture (measure first and then squeeze)
- 2 large cloves garlic, grated
- ½ teaspoon dried oregano
- ¼ teaspoon ground black pepper

**Directions:**

1. Preheat the oven to 350°F. Place a sheet of parchment paper on a large baking sheet.
2. Spray the paper with cooking oil spray.

3. Combine meat, egg, zucchini, and seasonings in a bowl. Make sure not to over-mix.

4. Make 23 equal portions of the mixture and shape into balls. Place on the baking sheet and bake for 20 – 25 minutes or until brown on the outside and cooked through inside. Turn the balls over every 7 – 8 minutes.

5. Serve hot. You can store the leftover meatballs in an airtight container in the refrigerator for about 5 days or in the freezer for about 3 months. If you freeze them, thaw them completely, reheat and serve.

## Salted Caramel Energy Balls

Serves: 18

Nutritional values per serving: 1 ball

Calories: 100

Fat: 5 g

Carbohydrates: 14 g

Protein: 2 g

**Ingredients:**

- 24 dates, pitted
- 3 tablespoons warm water

- ¾ teaspoon vanilla extract
- 3 tablespoons coarsely chopped, toasted pecans
- 6 tablespoons sunflower seed butter
- ¾ teaspoon kosher salt
- 1 cup rolled oats
- ¼ cup shredded coconut

**Directions:**

1. Add dates, water, vanilla, sunflower seed butter, and salt into a food processor bowl and process until most of it is smooth but not completely smooth.
2. Remove the mixture into a bowl. Stir in oats and pecans.
3. Make 18 equal portions of the mixture and shape each into a ball. Moisten your hands with some water while forming the balls.
4. Next, dredge the balls in shredded coconut and serve.
5. You can store the leftover balls in an airtight container in the refrigerator for about 5 days or in the freezer for about 3 months.

## Mini Shepherd's Pie Muffins

Serves: 6

Nutritional values per serving: 1 muffin

Calories: 110

Fat: 3.69 g

Carbohydrates: 7.88 g

Protein: 6.9 g

**Ingredients:**

For broccoli mashed potatoes:

- 1 large Russet potato, peeled, cubed
- 1/8 cup milk of your choice
- 1/8 cup shredded cheese of your choice
- ¾ cup roughly chopped broccoli florets
- ½ tablespoon butter

For meat filling:

- 1 small onion, finely chopped
- ½ cup frozen mixed vegetables
- ½ teaspoon dried thyme

- 1 small egg, beaten
- 1 teaspoon olive oil
- 1 clove garlic, minced
- ½ pound lean ground beef
- ½ tablespoon tomato paste
- ½ teaspoon Worcestershire sauce (optional)

**Directions:**

1. For broccoli mashed potatoes: Pour 2 inches of water into a pot. Place the potato cubes in a steamer basket and steam in the pot for 10 minutes.
2. Scatter the broccoli over the potatoes and continue steaming until the vegetables are very soft.
3. Take out vegetables and add them to a bowl. Add milk, cheese, and butter and mash well to the desired texture.
4. To make the filling: Set the oven temperature to 375° F and preheat the oven. Prepare 6 ramekins by greasing them with some cooking spray.
5. Pour oil into a pan and let it heat over medium heat. When oil is hot, add garlic and onion and cook for a minute.
6. Stir in carrots and cook for 4–5 minutes, stirring occasionally.

7. Stir in tomato paste. Turn off the heat. Remove the vegetables from the pan and add to a bowl. Add beef, Worcestershire sauce, and egg and mix until just combined. Ensure you do not over-mix, or the meat will become tough.
8. Distribute the mixture into the ramekins.
9. Distribute the mash equally and spread it over the meat mixture in the ramekins.
10. Place the ramekins in the oven and set the timer for 25 to 30 minutes or until golden brown.
11. Serve hot for adults and warm for baby.

## Apple And Peanut Butter Sandwiches

Serves: 6

Nutritional values per serving: 1 sandwich without toppings

Calories: 126

Fat: 8 g

Carbohydrates: 12 g

Protein: 4 g

**Ingredients:**

- 2 apples, cored, cut each into 6 slices
- toppings of your choice (optional)
- 6 tablespoons natural peanut butter

**Directions:**

1. Cut the apple into slices crosswise. The slices should have the cored part in the center of the slice.
2. Place 6 apple slices on a serving platter. Spread a tablespoon of peanut butter over each slice. Scatter the chosen toppings if using. Cover each with a slice of apple to complete the sandwich.

## Banana Oatmeal Cookies

Serves: 4

Nutritional values per serving: 2 cookies

Calories: 93

Fat: 3.5 g

Carbohydrates: 15 g

Protein: 2 g

**Ingredients:**

- 1 medium ripe banana, mashed

- 1/8 cup crushed walnuts
- ½ cup rolled oats

**Directions:**

1. Set the temperature of the oven to 350° F and preheat the oven. Grease a baking sheet with some olive oil cooking spray.
2. If desired, slightly powder the oats in a blender.
3. Add banana and oats into a bowl and mix well. Add walnuts and stir.
4. Scoop out 8 equal portions of the mixture and place on the baking sheet.
5. Place the baking sheet in the oven and bake for 15 minutes or until golden brown around the edges.

**Desserts:**

## Brownie Bites

Serves: 11

Nutritional values per serving: 1 bite

Calories: 92

Fat: 4 g

Carbohydrates: 14 g

Protein: 2 g

**Ingredients:**

- 1 medium, very ripe banana
- 1 tablespoon coconut oil
- 1/8 cup cacao powder
- 1/8 cup cacao nibs
- 4 medjool dates, pitted, chopped
- ½ medium avocado, peeled, pitted, chopped
- ¼ teaspoon pure vanilla extract
- ½ cup rolled or old-fashioned oats
- 1/8 cup chia seeds
- cocoa powder to garnish (optional)
- coconut flakes, unsweetened to dredge (optional)

**Directions:**

1. Combine avocado, banana, vanilla, and oil in a bowl. Mash the mixture completely.

2. Make 11 equal portions of the mixture and shape into balls. Dredge the balls in coconut flakes if desired. Sprinkle cocoa powder on top if using.
3. Place in a glass airtight container in the refrigerator. It can last for about 10 days. You can freeze it in a freezer-safe container in the freezer for about 3 months.

## Gingerbread Date Balls

Serves: 30

Nutritional values per serving: 1 ball without pecans

Calories: 43

Fat: 0 g

Carbohydrates: 11 g

Protein: 0 g

**Ingredients:**

- 16 ounces pitted dates
- ¼ teaspoon ground nutmeg
- 1/8 teaspoon ground cloves
- ½ teaspoon ground cinnamon

- 1/8 teaspoon ground allspice
- 1/8 teaspoon ground ginger

To dredge: Optional

- finely chopped pecans

**Directions:**

1. Place dates and spices in the mini food processor and process until the texture you desire is achieved. Scrape the sides of the mini food processor whenever required.
2. Moisten your hands with water, make 30 equal portions of the mixture, and shape into balls. You may have to moisten your hands often (after rolling 2 to 3 balls).
3. Dredge the balls in pecans and place them on a tray lined with parchment paper.
4. Chill for a few hours until it sets. Transfer the balls into an airtight container. Place it in the refrigerator. It can last for a week.

## Pumpkin Pie Fudge

Serves: 12

Nutritional values per serving: 1 piece

Calories: 161

Fat: 12 g

Carbohydrates: 14 g

Protein: 2 g

**Ingredients:**

- 15 pitted Medjool dates
- ¼ cup pure pumpkin puree
- 1 teaspoon pumpkin pie spice
- ¼ cup natural, smooth peanut butter
- 3 tablespoons melted coconut oil

**Directions:**

1. Line a small loaf or baking pan with parchment or wax paper.
2. Place dates, pumpkin puree, pumpkin pie spice, peanut butter, and coconut oil in a blender and blend until smooth.
3. Pour the mixture into the prepared pan. Spread it evenly. Freeze for about 4 hours.
4. Remove the fudge from the pan and the parchment paper and place on your cutting board. Cut into 12 equal-sized pieces and serve.

5. Place leftover fudge in a freezer-safe container in the freezer. It can last for about a month.

## Chocolate Caramel Tarts

Serves: 6

Nutritional values per serving: 1 tart

Calories: 59

Fat: 8 g

Carbohydrates: 24 g

Protein: 2.5 g

**Ingredients:**

For the crust:

- ½ cup packed, soft, pitted dates
- ¼ cup unsweetened, finely shredded coconut
- ¼ cup chopped walnuts
- 1 tablespoon cocoa powder

For the filling:

- 1 ½ tablespoons natural peanut butter or almond butter
- a pinch of sea salt
- ¼ cup very tightly packed pitted dates
- 1 tablespoon full-fat coconut milk or coconut cream

**Directions:**

1. Soak the dates in a bowl of hot water for about 30 minutes.
2. Meanwhile, make the crust: Place walnuts and coconut in the mini food processor and give short pulses until chopped into smaller pieces.
3. Now add dates and cocoa and process until the mixture is crumbly.

4. Line a mini muffin pan of 6 counts with strips of parchment paper. Ensure the strips are long enough to pick them from the muffin cups.
5. Distribute the crust mixture equally and place it in the muffin cups. Press it onto the bottom and sides of the cups.
6. For the caramel: Discard the water from the bowl of dates and place it in the mini food processor. Add coconut milk, salt, and almond butter and process until smooth. Scrape the sides of the food processor whenever required.
7. Pour the caramel into the crusts. Top with shredded coconut.
8. Freeze for 35 to 40 minutes.
9. Now, pick up the tarts with the help of the extra parchment paper. Carefully peel off the parchment paper.
10. It is ready to serve now. Any remaining tarts can be stored in an airtight container in the refrigerator for a week or in the freezer for 3 months. Frozen ones need to be thawed for about 15 minutes and then served.

## Salted Caramel Tahini Cups

Serves: 18

Nutritional values per serving: 1 cup

Calories: 202

Fat: 13 g

Carbohydrates: 21.9 g

Protein: 2.6 g

**Ingredients:**

- 2/3 cup melted coconut oil
- 2 cups packed, pitted dates
- 1 cup smooth, drippy tahini
- ½ teaspoon sea salt

**Directions:**

1. Place dates in a pour. Cover the dates with hot water. Let them soak for 15 to 20 minutes.
2. Meanwhile, whisk together oil and tahini in a bowl.
3. Take 3 muffin pans of 6 counts each and place disposable liners in each cup. Place 1 tablespoon of the coconut oil mixture in each cup.
4. Freeze until firm, about 10 – 12 minutes.
5. Now drain the water from the dates, place in a blender along with salt, and blend until smooth. Scrape the sides of the blender whenever required.

6. Distribute equally the blended dates among the muffin cups and place them over the tahini layer.
7. Freeze until firm. Remove from the muffin pan and place in an airtight container in the refrigerator for about a week or in the freezer for about 2 months.

## Berries Cottage Cheese Ice Cream

Serves: 2

Nutritional values per serving: ½ recipe, without toppings

Calories: 125

Fat: 3 g

Carbohydrates: 20 g

Protein: 6 g

**Ingredients:**

- ¾ cup frozen berries of your preference
- ½ cup low-fat cottage cheese or lactose-free cottage cheese
- ¼ cup sliced ripe banana
- 2 pitted dates

Topping suggestions:

- fresh berries
- banana slices
- nuts
- pureed berries

**Directions:**

1. Place berries, cottage cheese, banana, and dates in a blender and blend until smooth.
2. If the dates are not soft, soak them in hot water for 15 minutes. Drain off the water and use the dates.
3. Transfer the blended mixture into a freezer-safe container and freeze until you can scoop.
4. Scoop into bowls and serve. You can store leftover ice cream in an airtight container in the refrigerator. It can last for about 20 – 25 days.

## Strawberry Banana N'ice Cream

Serves: 12

Nutritional values per serving: 1/12 recipe

Calories: 110

Fat: 0.62 g

Carbohydrates: 20 g

Protein: 7 g

**Ingredients:**

- 6 bananas, chopped into chunks, frozen
- 2 teaspoons vanilla extract
- 24 ounces frozen strawberries (about 4 ½ cups)
- 1 cup unsweetened almond milk or coconut milk

**Directions:**

1. Blend bananas, vanilla, strawberries, and almond milk in the food processor bowl or a blender until smooth. Scrape the sides of the bowl whenever required.
2. Scoop and serve immediately for a soft-serve ice cream.
3. To freeze: Line a baking sheet with parchment paper. Scoop out the ice cream and place it on the baking sheet.
4. Freeze until firm. Now, transfer the scoops of ice cream into a Ziploc bag and freeze until used.
5. To serve, remove the required number of scoops from the bag and place them in serving bowls. Let them thaw for a few minutes before enjoying.

## Raspberry and Banana Mousse

Serves: 2

Nutritional values per serving: 1 bowl

Calories: 122

Fat: 0.2 g

Carbohydrates: 19.5 g

Protein: 11.3 g

**Ingredients:**

- 4 egg whites
- 4 ounces frozen bananas
- fresh raspberries to serve (optional)
- 3 ½ ounces frozen raspberry

**Directions:**

1. Beat the egg whites in a blender until stiff. When you upturn the blender, the whites should not drop off.
2. Next, add raspberries and bananas and blend until very smooth.
3. Place a few fresh raspberries in each of the 2 serving bowls. Divide the mousse equally among the bowls.
4. Serve right away. Serving it later may deflate the mousse.

# Fig Newton's

Serves: 12

Nutritional values per serving: 1 cookie

Calories: 115

Fat: 5.5 g

Carbohydrates: 16.9 g

Protein: 2.1 g

**Ingredients:**

For the cookie dough:

- 1/8 cup oats
- ½ cup pecans
- ½ cup plus 1/8 cup firmly packed pitted dates
- ½ cup almonds
- 1/8 teaspoon sea salt

For the filling:

- 4 ounces dried black mission figs, discard stems
- 1/8 teaspoon ground cinnamon
- 5 pitted dates
- ½ teaspoon grated orange zest
- a tiny pinch of sea salt

**Directions:**

1. Set the temperature of the oven to 350° F and preheat the oven.

2. Spread oats, pecans, and almonds on a baking sheet and place it in the oven for 8 – 10 minutes. Make sure they do not burn. They should be light golden brown.
3. Take out the baking sheet and let it come to room temperature.
4. Transfer the contents of the baking sheet into a food processor bowl and add salt. Process until finely powdered.
5. Transfer onto a plate. Place dates in the food processor and process until smooth and it comes together.
6. Add nut mixture and give short pulses until the mixture can be shaped into a ball.
7. Place a sheet of parchment paper on your countertop. Place the dough on the parchment paper and cover with another parchment paper.
8. Roll the dough into a rectangle until it is ¼ inch thick.
9. Peel off the parchment paper. If necessary, re-shape into a rectangle using your hands.
10. Place figs in a bowl and pour hot water over the figs. Make sure the water is hot and not boiling. After 3 minutes, pick out the figs, but do not discard the soaking water.
11. Place figs, cinnamon, orange zest, and salt in the food processor and process until well combined. Add the date-

soaked water a teaspoon and process each time until you get a thick paste. Make sure not to add excess water.

12. Add dates and process until smooth.
13. Next, spoon the mixture all along the center of the rectangle, spreading only a 1-inch area all along the center. You can say 1-inch-thick line.
14. Now fold both sides over the filling such that both sides meet together. Use the help of the parchment paper to lift. It may break a little while doing so, but that's okay. Pinch the cracked part to smoothen and seal the edges as well. So now you have a log.
15. Line a tray with parchment paper and place the log on it. Place in the freezer for at least a couple of hours.
16. Cut into 12 equal slices and serve. You can save the leftovers in an airtight container in the refrigerator for a week.

## Chocolate Truffles

Serves: 8

Nutritional values per serving: 1 truffle

Calories: 84

Fat: 3.5 g

Carbohydrates: 13.1 g

Protein: 1.5 g

**Ingredients:**

- 1 tablespoon water
- 3.2 ounces pitted Medjool dates
- ¼ teaspoon vanilla extract
- a pinch of sea salt
- ½ tablespoon coconut oil
- 1/8 cup unsweetened cacao powder plus extra for dredging
- ¾ tablespoon cashew butter, almond butter, or sunflower seed butter
- 4 – 6 tablespoons almond flour

**Directions:**

1. Prepare a small plate by lining it with parchment paper.
2. Place dates, water, and coconut oil in the mini food processor and process until you get a paste.
3. Next goes the vanilla, salt, cacao, and cashew butter into the food processor. Process until well combined.
4. Add 2 tablespoons of almond flour and mix well. Add another 2 tablespoons and mix well. You need sticky

dough, but that can be formed into balls. So, add only 1 to 2 tablespoons of almond flour if required.

5. Make 8 equal portions of the dough and shape each into a ball. It may be difficult to form the balls as the dough is sticky.
6. You can moisten your hands with some water while forming the balls.
7. Dredge the balls in cacao powder. Place the balls on the prepared plate. If you like the balls to be soft, you can enjoy them now. If you like firm balls, freeze them for 30 minutes.
8. Place the balls in an airtight container in the refrigerator for about a week or in the freezer for about a month.

## Pumpkin Caramels

Serves: 10

Nutritional values per serving: 1 caramel

Calories: 80

Fat: 2.8 g

Carbohydrates: 13.9 g

Protein: 1.5 g

**Ingredients:**

- 6 ounces Medjool dates, pitted, soaked in hot water for 10 minutes if the dates are not sticky
- ½ teaspoon pumpkin pie spice
- ¼ teaspoon sea salt
- 1 tablespoon pumpkin butter or pumpkin puree
- 1 tablespoon melted coconut oil
- 3 tablespoons toasted pepitas

**Directions:**

1. Process the dates in the food processor until you can shape them into balls.
2. Blend in the pumpkin butter, pumpkin pie spice, and salt. Pour the oil into a thin stream through the feeder tube with the blender machine running. Process until well combined.
3. Remove the mixture into a bowl. Place in the freezer for about 3 – 4 hours.
4. Make 10 equal portions of the mixture and shape into balls. Dredge the balls in pepitas. Press slightly when you dredge so the pepitas will adhere to the balls.

5. Sprinkle salt on top of the balls and place on a plate lined with parchment paper. Freeze until firm. Once frozen, transfer into a freezer-safe container and freeze until use.
6. You can serve them frozen or slightly thawed.

# Simple, Quick Recipes for Busy People

## Cauliflower Chicken Fried Rice

Serves: 2

Nutritional values per serving: 1 ½ cups

Calories: 305

Fat: 16 g

Carbohydrates: 12 g

Protein: 30 g

**Ingredients:**

- 3 ½ teaspoons vegetable oil, divided
- ½ tablespoon sesame oil (optional)
- 2 small scallions, thinly sliced; keep the green and white parts separate
- 2 cloves garlic, minced
- ¼ cup diced red bell pepper
- ½ pound chicken breasts, skinless, boneless, diced

- pepper to taste
- 1 large egg, beaten
- ½ tablespoon grated fresh ginger
- ½ cup snow peas, trimmed, halved
- salt to taste
- 2 cups cauliflower rice
- 1 ½ tablespoons soy sauce or tamari

**Directions:**

1. Cauliflower rice is cauliflower florets grated to a rice-like texture. You can do this using a box grater or buy store-bought ones.
2. Place a pan over high heat. Add ½ teaspoon vegetable oil. When the oil is hot, pour the beaten egg and do not stir.
3. When the underside is cooked, turn the omelet over and cook the other side for a few seconds.
4. Remove the omelet from the pan and place on your cutting board. Cut into strips.
5. Add 1 ½ teaspoons of peanut oil to the pan. Add ginger, whites of the scallions, and garlic, and cook for a few seconds until slightly soft.

6. Stir in the salt, chicken, and pepper. After about a minute, add bell pepper and snow peas.
7. Stir on and off for about 5 minutes. Remove the chicken mixture onto a plate.
8. Add the remaining oil to the pan. Add cauliflower rice to the hot oil. Heat thoroughly for about 2 minutes.
9. Mix well with the chicken mixture, soy sauce, omelet strips, and sesame oil.
10. Cook for a couple of minutes. Turn off the heat.
11. Add scallions and give it a good stir.
12. Serve hot.

## Roasted Chicken and Vegetables

Serves: 3

Nutritional values per serving: 1/3 recipe

Calories: 370

Fat: 24 g

Carbohydrates: 22 g

Protein: 18 g

**Ingredients:**

- ½ tablespoon balsamic vinegar
- 1 tablespoon chopped fresh thyme or basil or 1 teaspoon dried thyme or basil
- ¼ teaspoon salt or to taste
- 1 pound chicken breasts or drumsticks or thighs, skinless
- ½ large red onion cut into 1-inch wedges
- 2 medium potatoes, peeled, cut into 1-inch cubes
- 1 cup cherry tomatoes
- 3 cloves garlic, minced
- ½ cup kalamata olives
- ½ red bell pepper, chopped into 1-inch squares
- 2 tablespoons extra-virgin olive oil, divided
- ¼ freshly ground black pepper
- ½ teaspoon smoked paprika

**Directions:**

1. Preheat the oven to 400° F.
2. Add ½ of each -oil, pepper, garlic, paprika, and salt into a bowl and mix. Smear this mixture over the chicken.

3. Combine potatoes, tomatoes, onion, olives, and bell pepper in a bowl.
4. Add the remaining half of each - pepper, garlic, paprika, salt, and oil and give the vegetables a good stir.
5. Place the vegetables in a baking dish and the chicken over the vegetables.
6. Place the baking dish in the oven and roast until the vegetables are tender and the chicken is cooked. The internal temperature of the chicken in the thickest part should show 165° F on the meat thermometer.
7. Garnish with basil or thyme. Serve chicken and vegetables with the cooked juices drizzled on top.

## Crispy Chicken Thighs with White Beans

Serves: 2

Nutritional values per serving: ½ recipe

Calories: 423

Fat: 26.9 g

Carbohydrates: 22 g

Protein: 23 g

**Ingredients:**

- 1 tablespoon olive oil, divided
- ½ teaspoon kosher salt, divided
- ½ cup finely chopped red onion
- ½ can (from a 15-ounce can) of unsalted cannellini beans, with their liquid
- 2 chicken thighs, skin-on boneless
- 1/8 teaspoon freshly ground black pepper
- ½ Fresno pepper, thinly sliced
- 3 tablespoons prepared pesto

**Directions:**

1. Add ½ tablespoon of oil into a skillet over high heat.
2. Season chicken with pepper and 1/8 teaspoon of salt and place in the skillet with the skin side facing down. Let it cook for 2 minutes.
3. Turn down the heat to medium-high. Place a heavy skillet on top of the chicken. Use a couple of bean cans if you do not have a heavy pan.
4. When the skins turn crisp, remove the heavy skillet, turn the chicken over, and cook the other side for 2 minutes.
5. Transfer the chicken onto a plate and set aside.

6. Turn up the heat to high heat. Add the remaining oil to the skillet. Stir the onions and pepper into the hot oil and cook until the onions are slightly golden brown.
7. Add beans and cook for 2 minutes.
8. Add remaining salt and pesto.
9. Mix well.
10. Serve crispy chicken thighs with pesto beans and serve.

## Pumpkin Soup

Serves: 4

Nutritional values per serving: ¼ recipe

Calories: 114

Fat: 8 g

Carbohydrates: 8 g

Protein: 3 g

**Ingredients:**

- 1 tablespoon olive oil
- 1 tablespoon minced fresh ginger
- ½ tablespoon minced garlic

- ½ small jalapeño chili, deseeded, finely chopped
- ½ teaspoon grated lime zest
- ½ can (from a 15.5 ounces can) light coconut milk
- salt to taste
- ½ large onion, chopped
- ½ can (from 15 ounces) of pumpkin puree
- 2 cups broth

**Directions:**

1. Add oil to a pan and place it over medium heat. Add onions and ginger and stir often until the onion turns pink. Add jalapeño and garlic and cook for a couple of minutes stirring often.
2. Add coconut milk, salt, pumpkin puree, lime zest, broth, and stir. Turn down the heat to medium-low and simmer for 15 minutes. Turn off the heat.
3. Cool for a while and blend with an immersion blender.
4. Heat the soup if desired. Ladle into soup bowls and serve.

## Chicken Florentine

Serves: 2

Nutritional values per serving: 1 ½ cups

Calories: 375

Fat: 18 g

Carbohydrates: 9 g

Protein: 39 g

**Ingredients:**

- 1 tablespoon extra-virgin olive oil, divided
- ¼ teaspoon salt, divided
- 1/8 cup finely chopped shallot
- 3 tablespoons dry white wine
- 3 tablespoons heavy cream
- ½ pound chicken breasts, thinly sliced
- ¼ teaspoon pepper, divided
- 1 large clove garlic, minced
- ½ pound baby spinach
- 1 teaspoon cornstarch

**Directions:**

1. Add ½ tablespoon of oil into a skillet and place it over medium-high heat.
2. Sprinkle 1/8 teaspoon each of salt and pepper over the chicken and place in the skillet.
3. Cook for about 4 minutes on each side or until well-cooked inside.
4. Remove the chicken from the skillet and place on a plate. Cover the chicken with foil and let it rest.
5. Pour ½ tablespoon of oil into the same skillet. Turn down the heat to medium heat.
6. Add garlic and shallot and stir. Cook for a few seconds until you get a nice aroma.
7. Stir in the wine. Scrape the bottom of the skillet to remove any particles that are stuck.
8. Stir in the spinach. Cook for about 3 minutes.
9. Combine cornstarch, cream, remaining salt, and pepper in a bowl and pour into the skillet.
10. Stir constantly until the sauce is thick.
11. Serve chicken with sauce.

## Quesadillas

Serves: 4

Nutritional values per serving: 1 wedge, without optional ingredients

Calories: 288.5

Fat: 22.9 g

Carbohydrates: 9.8 g

Protein: 20.4 g

**Ingredients:**

- 2 low-carb tortillas
- ¾ teaspoon chili powder
- 1/8 teaspoon dried oregano
- ½ teaspoon ground cumin
- 1/8 teaspoon pepper
- ¼ teaspoon crushed red pepper flakes or to taste
- ¼ teaspoon paprika or to taste
- ¼ teaspoon salt
- 2 small cloves garlic, minced

- 1 ½ teaspoons butter, divided
- ½ cup grated mozzarella or cheddar cheese, or use a mixture of both
- 4 ounces ground beef
- 1/8 cup water
- 1 green onion, thinly sliced
- ¼ avocado, peeled, pitted, sliced

*For toppings: (Optional)*

- chopped tomatoes
- sour cream
- sliced green onions

**Directions:**

1. Add beef into a skillet and place it over medium heat. Stir often until it turns brown. As you stir, break the meat into crumbles.
2. Drain off the cooked fat from the skillet. Add garlic and all the spices and give it a good stir.
3. Cook for about a minute, stirring often. Add water and mix well. Cook until the water is gone.
4. Remove the skillet and place a nonstick pan over low heat.

5. Add half the butter to the pan. Let the butter melt. Swirl the pan to spread the butter.
6. Place a tortilla in the pan. Sprinkle cheese all over the tortilla. Spread the beef mixture over the tortilla, followed by green onion and avocado.
7. Place another tortilla on top. Press gently. When the underside is crisp and brown, turn the quesadilla over and cook the other side.
8. Remove the quesadilla onto a plate. Cut into 4 equal wedges.
9. Serve topped with any of the suggested toppings if desired.

## Avocado Tuna Spinach Salad

Serves: 2

Nutritional values per serving: ½ recipe

Calories: 432

Fat: 32 g

Carbohydrates: 17 g

Protein: 20 g

**Ingredients:**

- 1 can (5 ounces) water-packed tuna
- ½ cup halved cherry tomatoes
- 1/8 cup diced red onion
- 4 cups baby spinach
- ½ cup diced avocado
- 3 tablespoons poppy seed dressing
- 2 tablespoons extra-virgin olive oil
- 1/8 cup sunflower seeds to garnish

**Directions:**

1. Place 2 cups spinach on each of 2 serving plates.
2. Add tuna, tomatoes, onion, avocado, oil, and dressing into a bowl and mix well. Divide the salad equally and place it over the spinach.
3. Serve.

## Chicken and Mushrooms

Serves: 3

Nutritional values per serving: 1/3 recipe, without serving options

Calories: 245

Fat: 10 g

Carbohydrates: 4 g

Protein: 33 g

**Ingredients:**

- 2 boneless, skinless chicken breasts, cut into 2-inch pieces
- 1 clove garlic, grated
- ¼ teaspoon dried oregano
- ¼ teaspoon pepper
- ¼ teaspoon smoked paprika
- ¼ teaspoon salt
- ½ large onion, sliced
- 4 ounces brown mushrooms, sliced
- 1 tablespoon unsalted butter
- ½ tablespoon extra-virgin olive oil
- a handful of fresh parsley leaves, finely chopped

To serve: Optional

- mashed potatoes

- salad

**Directions:**

1. Place a cast-iron skillet over medium-high heat. When the skillet is nice and hot, pour the oil into the skillet. Place chicken in the skillet.
2. Combine the seasonings in a bowl and sprinkle over the chicken.
3. Cook the chicken until brown on both sides and cooked through inside.
4. Transfer the chicken onto a plate.
5. Add butter to the skillet. When the butter melts, add onion and mushrooms and stir. Cook until the vegetables are tender. Remove from heat.
6. Mix the chicken with the onion mixture. Stir in parsley and garlic.
7. Serve as it is or with any of the suggested serving options.

## Cod and Asparagus Bake

Serves: 2

Nutritional values per serving: ½ recipe

Calories: 141

Fat: 3 g

Carbohydrates: 6 g

Protein: 23 g

**Ingredients:**

- 2 cod fillets (4 ounces each)
- 1 cup cherry tomatoes, halved
- ¾ teaspoon grated lemon zest
- ½ pound fresh thin asparagus, trimmed
- 1 tablespoon lemon juice
- 1/8 cup grated Romano cheese

**Directions:**

1. Preheat oven to 375° F. Grease a baking dish with some oil.
2. Place the tomato halves in the baking dish with the cut side touching the bottom. Place the asparagus as well.
3. Place fish in the baking dish on top of the vegetables. Brush lemon juice over the fish. Scatter lemon zest on the fish.
4. Sprinkle cheese over the fish as well as the vegetables. Place the baking dish in the oven and bake for 12 minutes

or until the fish is cooked. If you pierce a fork into the fish, it should flake.

5. Take out the baking dish and set the oven to broil mode. Preheat the broiler.
6. Place the baking dish back in the oven and broil for a few minutes until the vegetables are light brown.

## Pan Roasted Potatoes

Serves: 2

Nutritional values per serving: ½ recipe

Calories: 141

Fat: 3 g

Carbohydrates: 9 g

Protein: 5 g

**Ingredients:**

- ½ pound fingerling or new red potatoes rinsed
- ½ yellow onion, thinly sliced
- 5 whole sage leaves
- ½ tablespoon olive oil

- 1 clove garlic, minced (use more garlic if you like garlic flavor)
- ½ teaspoon red pepper flakes or to taste
- salt to taste

**Directions:**

1. Place potatoes in a pot. Add a little salt and cover with water.
2. Place the pot over high heat. Boil until the potatoes are tender and can be pierced with a fork.
3. Drain the potatoes in a colander and rinse with cold water. Drain well.
4. Pour oil into a nonstick pan and place it over medium-high heat. Add onion and stir often for a couple of minutes.
5. Stir in the garlic and cook until the onion turns light brown.
6. Add sage and cook until it wilts. Stir in the potatoes. Now, do not disturb the potatoes until the underside is brown. Turn the potatoes over and similarly cook the other sides until brown.
7. Serve.

## Sweet Potato, Kale, and Shrimp Skillet

Serves: 2

Nutritional values per serving: ½ recipe

Calories: 265

Fat: 7.8 g

Carbohydrates: 18 g

Protein: 32.1 g

**Ingredients:**

- ½ teaspoon red pepper flakes or to taste (optional)
- salt to taste
- pepper to taste
- 1 tablespoon extra-virgin olive oil or ghee
- 1 clove garlic, minced
- ¼ cup diced onion
- 1 cup diced sweet potatoes
- 1 ½ cups coarsely chopped kale leaves
- 1 cup shrimp, peeled, deveined, defrosted if using frozen

**Directions:**

1. Add oil into a cast iron skillet and place it over medium heat.
2. When the oil is hot, add onion and cook until the onion turns light golden brown. Add garlic and red pepper and cook for a few seconds until you get a nice aroma.
3. Stir in the sweet potatoes. Sprinkle some water and cover the skillet. Cook until the sweet potatoes are fork tender.
4. Stir in the shrimp. Once they turn pink, in about 2 to 3 minutes, stir in the kale.
5. Cook until the kale turns limp. Add seasonings and mix well.
6. Serve.

## Grilled Tilapia Piccata

Serves: 2

Nutritional values per serving: 1 fillet

Calories: 206

Fat: 8 g

Carbohydrates: 2 g

Protein: 32 g

**Ingredients:**

- ¼ teaspoon grated lemon zest
- 1 tablespoon olive oil
- 1 teaspoon drained capers
- 2 tilapia fillets (6 ounces each)
- 1/8 teaspoon pepper
- 1 ½ tablespoons lemon juice
- 1 clove garlic, minced
- 4 fresh basil leaves, minced, divided
- ¼ teaspoon salt

**Directions:**

1. Set the oven to broil mode and preheat the oven to medium heat.
2. Meanwhile, combine lemon juice, zest, garlic, and oil in a bowl. Add half the basil and capers and mix well.
3. Set aside a tablespoon of this mixture and brush the rest on either side of the fillets. Season the fillets with salt and pepper.

4. Place on a baking sheet in the oven, 4 inches below the heating element. Broil for 3 to 4 minutes on either side or until cooked through.
5. Spoon the retained lemon juice mixture over the fillets. Garnish with remaining basil and serve.

## Turkey Skillet Dinner with Sweet Potatoes and Kale

Serves: 3

Nutritional values per serving: 1/3 recipe

Calories: 373

Fat: 18 g

Carbohydrates: 18 g

Protein: 32 g

**Ingredients:**

- 1 tablespoon olive oil
- ½ small onion, diced
- 1 ½ cups chopped kale or spinach
- salt to taste

- pepper to taste
- 1-pound lean ground turkey
- 1 ½ cups peeled sweet potato chunks
- 1/8 cup crumbled goat cheese
- chopped parsley to garnish (optional)

**Directions:**

1. Add oil into a skillet and place it over medium heat. When the oil is hot, add onion and cook until pink.
2. Stir in the turkey. As you stir, break into crumbles. Cook until turkey turns brown.
3. Stir in the sweet potatoes and a sprinkle of water. Cook covered until the sweet potato is tender.
4. Stir in the kale. Cook for a few minutes until kale turns limp.
5. Mix in the cheese and serve garnished with parsley.

## Greek Turkey Taco Lettuce Wraps

Serves: 2

Nutritional values per serving: 3 wraps

Calories: 126

Fat: 8 g

Carbohydrates: 10 g

Protein: 6 g

**Ingredients:**

- ½ pound ground turkey
- ½ tablespoon olive oil
- 6 butter lettuce leaves
- ½ large cucumber, chopped
- ¼ cup crumbled feta cheese
- 1 teaspoon Greek seasoning or more to taste (or use Italian seasoning)
- 1 teaspoon minced garlic
- ¼ red onion chopped
- 12 cherry tomatoes, halved

**Directions:**

1. Place a skillet over medium heat. Add turkey and cook until it does not look pink anymore. Stir on and off. As you stir, break the meat into crumbles.

2. Stir in the Greek seasonings and cook for another 3 – 4 minutes.
3. Next, add the garlic and mix well. After about a minute, turn off the heat.
4. Place lettuce leaves on a serving plate. Divide the turkey mixture equally and place on the leaves.
5. Garnish with onion, tomatoes, cucumber, and feta and serve.

# Conclusion

Now, you don't have to restrict yourself to some soup diet or tiny meals just to lose weight. With the low carb Mediterranean diet, you will learn how to nourish your body properly while facilitating weight loss and other benefits. Following any fad diet that leaves you hungry or without energy throughout the day is not feasible. Crash dieting will make you binge eat and gain weight quicker.

Creating a sustainable and healthy relationship with food is the only thing that works in the long run. This is where this low carb Mediterranean diet cookbook comes in. Make smarter food choices and use the guidelines given by the low carb Mediterranean diet to lose weight and improve overall health. The recipes in this cookbook follow the diet's recommendations and will help you cook delicious food that is beneficial for your body. Start making a weekly meal plan using the low carb Mediterranean diet recipes, and you can stick to the diet effectively until you see results.

In time, you will notice how this diet benefits you with weight management alongside other aspects. Keeping this low carb Mediterranean cookbook handy will make integrating the diet into your daily life easier and support metabolic health while inducing weight loss. With the support of low carb Mediterranean diet supplements and healthy food, you will soon regain your health for good. Throw out those unhealthy snacks, go grocery shopping for healthy whole foods, and cook delicious low carb Mediterranean diet meals to see results soon.

Printed in Great Britain
by Amazon